Seeds of Love

Sowing in the Land of Albania

Written by

Glen and Sheila Watson

Arise Shine Albanian Ministry

For additional copies of this book
Or for more information about this ministry,
Please write or email:

Glen and Sheila Watson
Arise Shine Albanian Ministry.
P.O. Box 179
Lenoir City, TN 37771
junebugape@yahoo.com

Table of Contents

FORWARD……………………………………………………………………5

INTRODUCTION…………………………………………………………..8

1………………………SEEDS OF LOVE……………………………………10

2………………………NEW DOORS BEGIN TO OPEN……………….25

3……………………..THE SOWER SOWETH THE WORD…………54

4……………………..THE HEAVENS BEGIN TO OPEN! …………..82

5……………………..VISIONS BEGIN TO COME TO PASS………..93

6………………………EMAILS…………………………………………100

7………………………HE HATH DONE GREAT THINGS! ………..170

Dedication

We dedicate this book to all
Of those that have
Walked with us and prayed
For us on our journey
Especially, the Albanians.
To God be the Glory!

FORWARD

The following is a true story: In the winter of 1939 a little five pound baby boy was born in Vonore, Tennessee. He was the 8th child of fifteen. When he was approximately six years old his family moved to a farm in Loudon County. They were share croppers. One day, when he was around ten years old, he overheard his parents tell some visitors from Vonore the story about a lady named Mrs. Underwood. Mrs. Underwood used to give milk to their family. They didn't have any money to pay her. This happened before the little boy was ever born. His oldest sister was about six years old and she would walk by herself and carry approximately a gallon of milk home. It was a long walk. The boy heard this story several times while growing up. God was planting a seed in his heart for the future. When he asked some of his siblings if they remembered the story, no one remembered until he asked his oldest sister. She said, "Yes, I remember it because I am the one who carried the milk home!"

Over forty years later God enabled him to retire early. God sent him on missions' trips to Albania. He began to notice that many children didn't have any milk to drink. Something about it tugged at his heart and memory. Then the Holy Spirit brought to his remembrance the story he had first heard as a young boy. How a compassionate neighbor gave milk to his family when they were in need. A desire sprang up in his heart! It was the seed that had been planted so long ago in a young child's heart. God knew whose heart to plant the seed in....... the one He would call someday to do something about it. This is why the other children didn't recall the story. They were not the ones He would use for this particular mission.

After several years of traveling to Albania he shared his heart's desire with a fellow believer. We will call him Mr. B. He told Mr. B that he would like to give a needy family a milk cow before he took his final trip to Albania. Mr. B shared this desire with Mr. J and other believers in his church. God moved on the hearts of these believers and they began giving for the milk cows. Upon returning from a trip to Florida, the man was very surprised to receive donations from these believers. He had planned on buying a cow himself but now God had enabled him to buy more than one cow! When he shared his joy about the donations with friends in his hometown, they got excited and decided they wanted to buy a cow, too! Mrs. H said she wanted to buy a fat cow!

Thanks to some believers joining with him, this man was able to bless four families not only with milk for a short while but for many years, as well as a means to earn some income.

The seed that was sown from one generous lady over sixty-five years ago has brought forth much fruit and is being sown again. This act of kindness made a big impression on one small boy. Maybe twenty, thirty years down the road there will be someone from Albania who will have a similar story to tell of a man that came from America and was used by God to provide for them during their time of need. Who knows maybe one of them will end up with a dairy full of cows, providing jobs for other needy families! It is amazing what one seed will bring forth.

Of course this small boy from Tennessee was Glen. He can truly say from experience that it is more blessed to give than receive. Thanks to many of you Glen and I have had the pleasure of blessing these families. We pray that God will multiply your seed many times over. You have not only given for cows but for food, clothing, school supplies, eyeglasses and medicine. We pray that God will richly reward you not only in the hereafter but in the right here and now! We love you all so much. Thank you for your prayers.

NOTE: Since first writing this story in 2003 the number of milk cows that have been given has grown from four to thirty-three! Praise God!

INTRODUCTION

Albania is a small nation about the size of Tennessee. It shares borders with Greece, Macedonia, Kosovo and Montenegro. They are descendants of the Illyrians which the Apostle Paul makes mention of in "**Rom 15:19** - Through mighty signs and wonders, by the power of the Spirit of God; so that from Jerusalem, and round about unto Illyricum, I have fully preached the gospel of Christ." Unfortunately, when the Turks invaded the land in 1385 most of the population was forced to convert to Islam. With the exception of about thirty-five years when their national hero, Skenderbeu, led a revolt. He was a Christian that temporarily gave his people freedom to worship Jesus Christ.

In recent history, they were ruled by a strong Stalinist variety of communism under a dictator name Enver Hoxha. He eventually cut his people off from contact with all nations including other communist nations. In 1967, Albania became the first nation in history to declare itself officially atheistic. After the dictator's death in 1985, communism began to decline. By 1992 Albanians elected a democratic government. This is where our story begins.

Read how God took a farm boy from the hills of Tennessee with very little formal education and enabled him to walk freely and without fear among the Muslim people of Albania. Although he had little formal education, God had prepared him well for what He was calling him to do. He knew he wasn't trained to be a minister of the Gospel and so he had to be totally dependent on God for each step he took.

He hopes this will encourage people from all walks of life to step out in faith and obey God. It will be the most exciting, thrilling and fulfilling life you could hope for.

If apostle means "sent one" then I would have to call my husband an "apostle of love" because that is what he has been doing in Albania for the past seventeen years.

SEEDS OF LOVE

Chapter 1

1993

IN THE BEGINNING

Sheila and I went to an Open Doors Prayer Conference in 1990 in Atlanta, Ga. My wife and I had been Bible couriers in 1988 and 1989 to two communist countries. During a meeting they discussed they needed Bibles for Albania but didn't have them printed yet. When they told us about the need I started weeping about Albania. I didn't even know where Albania was located. I went home and looked it up on a world map. My friend, George Simon was helping us look for it and found it first. He said, "There it is on the Adriatic Sea." It was the first time I had ever heard of the Adriatic. I knew in my heart that God was calling me to Albania. I started saving money to go to Albania when the opportunity arose. By 1992 I was making plans to retire when I finished my job in Arkansas. I started calling different ministries trying to get information. I called Open Doors to see if they had Bibles that I could take in but they still didn't have any yet. I made contact with a woman in Colorado Springs who put me in touch with two men that were planning a trip in March of 1993. They were both from John Osteen's church. I don't remember their full names. One man was Mike and the other man's name was Sammy Tibbons.

We had never met. I met them the first time at the Atlanta airport. When I got to the airport a big man walked up to me, put out his hand and said, "Are you Watson?" I replied, "Yes." While we were waiting for our plane we sat down and began to exchange information we had. I told them they needed to make copies of their passports because someone had advised me to do this because they would try to steal your passport and sell it on the black market for $3000. They made copies while we waited.

We flew to Zurich, Switzerland and changed planes to fly in to Albania. When we were approaching Albania we began to look out the window. We were flying over the Adriatic Sea and as we approached the airport we had to circle back around because there were some sheep on the runway. They didn't have radar at the time. When we got off the airplane we had to walk about 500 feet to the terminal. After we went through customs, we caught a cab and went to Tirana Hotel. We got a room for one night. We didn't know anyone. We were all going to spy the land out. The next morning we met in the lobby and began looking for transportation, translator and lodging. We began asking around and finally met a man from Hungary. We couldn't pronounce his name so we called him "Trouble". Trouble had about a two and half ton milk truck with no windows. We hired him to take us around. He was a preacher. Trouble met a man that was trying to start a church in Shkodra which is north of Tirana. This was the first place we went. As we left Tirana we came to a split in the road. There wasn't any road sign. We could go left or right. Fortunately, we chose the correct road. As we went around the mountain we saw a cable bridge that connected two mountains to our right. There was a man on the bridge with a donkey. It was beautiful scenery with mountains on both sides and a big stream below him. It looked like he had groceries loaded on the donkey. It was in March and people were putting their gardens out.

You can stand in a castle in Shkodra and look over in to former Yugoslavia. They told us on the way up there that when they offer you something to eat or drink that you need to accept it or they would be offended. Sure enough they did. First they served us a small cup of coffee that was like sorghum molasses. After that they brought out some warm milk straight from the cow. One of them drank it but I just couldn't. Then we discussed having a little meeting at their house. We made plans to have it the next day. After leaving we got a bite to eat and split up into three groups and stayed in people's homes. Before the meeting our host wanted to serve us dinner. I had seen them killing a small lamb or goat. They were skinning it out. They chopped it up in small pieces about the size of your fist. It was cooked on an open fire. We had French fries and dried beans to go with it. Sammy Tibbons was the minister and was sitting next to me. They gave him the head because he was the honored guest. The eyeball was looking at us. Sammy offered it to me. I said, "No, brother. You are the honored guest." I had a pretty good piece of meat that looked like the neck bone. After we ate we had our meeting. There were about twenty-five people. The people were receptive but we didn't have any Bibles yet to give them. After the meeting we stood around and fellowshipped. We stayed a couple of hours just making friends. When we left we stayed in the same home as the night before. We paid ten dollars a night which included our meals. This should always be done because they will say "no" but it is only right because you are eating their food, etc... Also, in Albania it is rude to accept something at the first offer so you have to insist.

The next day we drove to Elbasan. We had a flat tire on a front wheel. We took one of the tires off the back (which had two tires on each wheel) and put it on the front. So now we were driving down the road a bit lopsided. We joyfully went on our way, not worrying about anything just singing and praising God. On the way we stopped at a small shop to get some snacks (not like ours!). As we were going across a one lane bridge the vehicle stopped. There was a hill behind and a hill in front of us. I said, "Which way are we going to push it?" One of the guys said, "It doesn't matter. Just push." Finally, it started and we continued on our way to Elbasan.

At last we arrived in Elbasan. Trouble knew a couple that was trying to start a church. We went to their house. They were from Chicago. The wife wasn't too happy with the Turkish toilet. She had a lid sitting over the hole. (These toilets are a ceramic square with a hole in the middle and they sit on the floor.) After talking about having some meetings we went for a walk. We bumped in to another American couple that was helping to get the church started. They had three sons and two of us stayed with them. While we were walking we bought some loaves of bread. The bread wasn't wrapped and I gave it to the boys to hold. They started eating on one of the loaves and the preacher from Chicago said they will have that whole loaf eaten before we get to their apartment. Sure enough they did. That night we had a service at a place they had rented.

One man came because he heard that some Americans were going to be there. He gave his testimony. Albania had just become free. He had heard about Jesus from someone and had been in prison because he was a Christian. He was from another communist country and when they released him they sent him to Albania because they didn't think he would survive there. We were in Elbasan three or four days meeting people, having meetings and just learning the culture. Then we headed back to Tirana.

When I returned I began looking for a place to live for a couple of months. I was looking for a private room with a private bath but that was not to be. My translator told me about a family that would let me live with them. They moved their two daughters out of their room and put them on the couch because they needed the money. I stayed in their room and shared the rest of the house. It worked out good because they would leave for school and work by 7 am. I would be gone before they returned. I would never eat there. I always ate out because I didn't want to be a hardship on them. I wanted to be a blessing to them.

My American friends returned to America after a couple of weeks. Now it was just me and Jesus (mostly, Jesus). I would go out during the day, getting to know the city. I saw where the college students would buy a hamburger and fries at a small outdoor stand for 90 lek (which was at that time about 75 cents). I would always leave the 10 lek for a tip which wasn't common at the time. I slowly began to find people that spoke some English. I began to venture out on buses or vans to other cities to get a feel for the country.

In the early mornings I would watch the city come to life. People would ride buses in to town and unload their produce from under the bus to sell at the produce market or on the sidewalk. People would set up little booths and sell whatever they could get.

Woman selling potatoes. She sat there all day.

They also brought in fresh milk in one liter, used, plastic “soft drink” bottles. I thought to myself, “This would be a good place to set up a milk factory” like they had in the fifties when they put milk in small bottles. I found out that this wouldn’t work there because the electricity was off as much as it was on. Also, the Holy Spirit impressed on me that this would stop all of the individuals from being able to sell their milk. I will tell more about this milk story a little later. This was the beginning of what the Holy Spirit was leading me to do.

Man selling fresh milk 1994

Foreign Christians began to flood in to Albania. Brother Andrew brought in the first full Bibles in the Albanian language. I was at the meeting when he presented the first Bible to political leaders. I didn't know that he would be in Albania when I made my first trip and have the joy to see him present the first Bible. It was just a special treat from my Lord and I praise Him for blessing me so. Of course, I had to buy some Bibles to give away! I bought a hundred and gave the first one to the family I was living with.

First Bibles I gave away in Albania

The Albanian people were open to the Gospel at this time. They had not had religious freedom for over forty years. The young people especially were hungry for “truth”. Christians began starting little prayer meetings and Bible studies all over the city. I started one in my room and hired a Christian from New Zealand to lead it.

Glen, Ina (lived with her family) and two others invited to my first Bible study.

After two months I returned to the states. While I was in the states I shared with people about Albania but most (at that time) were skeptical and not very interested. Some of my family thought that I was taking a vacation in Europe. By now it was June and I went to the Church of God camp meeting in Cleveland, Tennessee. I happened to sit down next to a man that was on the missions' board. We started to make small talk and he asked what I do. I told him that God had enabled me to retired that year at the age of 54 from the construction field and that I had just returned from a mission's trip to Albania where I was spying out the land. This got his interest because the Church of God had no one in Albania. He said, "I'll set you up a meeting with the missions' board." Shortly after that my wife and I met with them. I shared with them my plans and they wished me well and advised me to get in contact with their man over that area named Paul Lauster.

I began to prepare for a return trip in the fall. I loaded my suitcases with socks, clothing, shoes and some Tylenol. I also packed some Christian literature and music.

One day before I returned I went to the Waffle House in Lenoir City. Some friends of mine Bobby and Jackie were in there. When I shared about my upcoming trip Jackie gave me a hundred dollars to purchase Bibles. This was my first donation. Up until that time I had paid for everything from the money I had saved for missions. I thought I had enough money saved to go to Albania three times. I had a certain amount of money put aside for our living and I told the Lord that when I got down to that amount I wouldn't go anymore. That was seventeen years ago and I have been twice a year (with the exception of a couple of times).

On my second trip I stayed with the same family as before. I continued to make friends, give out Bibles, clothes, medicine and meet a need if the Lord put it in front of me. I worked with other missionaries if an opportunity arose. For instance, one time I went with a group that worked with Lester Sumrall. We took shoes and clothing by way of helicopter up in a mountain village. We landed in the school yard.

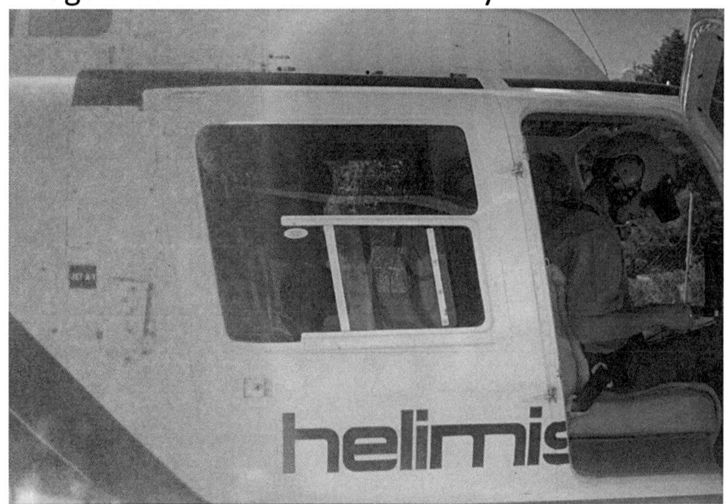

Glen in helicopter.

We had to fly low between the mountains. The Albanians would tell the missionaries what was needed and they would fly the items in on a return trip. They flew to different villages in Albania. The helicopter would drop us off and we would tell the pilot when to return. We would give out the supplies and then we would have a small Christian meeting. The supplies were stored in a big warehouse and the missionaries in charge lived in camper trailers that were also in the warehouse.

Warehouse and missionaries from Holland.

Chapter 2

1994

NEW DOORS BEGIN TO OPEN

As I mentioned earlier there was no Church of God anywhere in the country. There was an Assembly of God, Baptist, Church of Christ, Mormons, Jehovah Witness but no Church of God which is what I attended. These were all new churches because the country had only been open for a couple of years. When I returned in March of 1994 I brought an old friend and former pastor of mine from the Church of God with me. His name is Jack McKinley. He was my pastor in 1971 in Inglis, Florida when I met my wife Sheila. When we arrived in Tirana we went to an apartment I had rented before I left in the fall of 1993. It was cold in the apartment and Brother Jack wrapped up in a big blanket I gave him and said he slept like a bear. The next morning I took him around the city and showed him how the people lived.

During a time of prayer we felt impressed to try to find an Albanian believer who would be interested in helping us start a church. We didn't find anyone while Brother Jack was there, so I kept looking and praying. Then Paul Lauster, whom we had made contact with, who was over the Church of God missions for that part of the world flew in and I picked him up from the airport. He stayed in my apartment and I showed him around. I took him to a small church across from the Tirana Hotel. He greeted the people. We talked and Paul asked would I open an office for him in Tirana. It was located in my apartment.

First office for the Church of God in Albania.

I still had no minister, but after he left a lady told me about an evangelist preaching in a village. She said he was one of the best. When I heard him he was a little fireball like John the Baptist. He wasn't being paid. He was about nineteen years old and a former muslim. His name was Hervin Fushkati. Hervin was being trained by the muslims and he went to Christian meetings like a spy to disrupt them. He decided he needed to read the Bible so that he could present a good argument. While doing this he became a believer. At first his family was angry and made him leave his home. I invited him to my apartment to talk. His only transportation was a bicycle. I offered to hire him to start a church for $100 a month. He accepted my offer. Before I had left on this trip my wife had slipped two packs of one dollar bills in my suitcase with a note to use it where I felt led. It was a total of $100. When I would go through my suitcase I would move them aside. This was the first hundred dollars that was sown in to the church we were starting. I gave those two bundles of one dollar bills to Hervin. He stuffed them in his pocket and rode happily away on his bicycle.

Hervin and Glen in one of the first meetings.

The meetings were in my apartment and Hervin would stand in the doorway between two rooms and preach to the people in both rooms.

I called Paul Lauster and told him I had hired a young man to lead the church. I told him he was around nineteen years old. Brother Paul said, “Couldn’t you find someone older?” I explained that there wasn’t anyone older. Almost all of the believers in Albania had only been “born again” a couple of years. Most of them were children and teenagers. Even now, most of them are below the age of 35.

Our first service we had about thirty-five people. We didn’t have enough chairs and so Paul asked me to purchase some and they would reimburse me. I bought about twenty-five chairs.

We were off and running. The first “Church of God” had begun and I was praising God to be a part of what he was doing! After seventeen years my heart still rejoices.

Before I left I took Hervin to the bank and deposited enough money for him to withdraw his salary until I returned. His tithe was ten dollars so he would withdraw ninety and leave the other ten in there. I told him someone was going to have to trust someone so I was trusting him to do the right thing. When I returned in the fall, I saw in the bank book that he had been faithful to follow my instructions. God had led me to the right young man! "Great is thy faithfulness, O Lord to me."

****

We sold our house in February. We planned on doing some travelling around the country in our motorhome when I wasn't in Albania. It was the first time we didn't own our own home, except the one on wheels. When I returned to America my wife had the house emptied and ready for it's new owners. All of our children were out on their own. We have five children, Jerry, Mike, Glenda, Glen Jr. and April. Jerry, Glenda and Glen Jr. were living in Florida. April had just married and was living in Knoxville and Mike was living in Kentucky. When Sheila picked me up from the Atlanta airport we went and stayed in Barb and Herb Houghton's house. They always opened their home to us whenever we needed it. They were in Michigan at the time. We stayed there for a few weeks and then loaded the motorhome and headed west. We were going to a Church of God general assembly in San Antonio, Texas. We stopped on our way and went to our first Kenneth Copeland Believers Convention in Fort Worth, Texas. It was a wonderful time of refreshing and rejuvenating.

We were supposed to be in San Antonio at the end of the week for a missions meeting. This was the first time that Sheila met Paul Lauster and his wife Lilly. It was encouraging listening to the other missionaries sharing their adventures on the mission field. All the while my mind and heart were on Albania. I talked about Albania to everyone I met (and I still do).

We drove back to Tennessee and picked up our daughter April for a short trip to Florida before we returned to Albania. Sheila was planning on going with me this time. She wanted to see her family before leaving. While we were in Inverness, Florida I traded my motorhome. We took it to the beach for a few days. The girls enjoyed this. Sheila was dreading leaving April. By this time it was August and we were planning on leaving in September for two months.

Leaving behind her kids (especially April) was very difficult for her. She had left them for short mission trips but not for more than two weeks. It was only her love for Jesus that gave her the determination to go.

When we arrived back in Tennessee we parked our motorhome at the Houghtons' for a couple of days, then moved to an RV park in Knoxville for a week or so before leaving. We were planning on being in Albania for September and October. I decided to wash the windshield on the motorhome. I stood up on the hood of our VW and the next thing I knew I was under the motorhome. To this day I don't really know what happened. I know I slipped and that is all. Sheila was in the motorhome, about to dry her hair. She heard something and ran out to check on me. She heard me groaning under the motorhome. She called for help and someone called **911**. An ambulance took me to St. Mary's Hospital. I had broken my wrist so bad that I had to have surgery. I kept telling the surgeon that I was leaving for Albania in a week. After the surgery the doctor came out to speak to my wife, April and the Houghtons (who had rushed over as soon as Sheila called them). He told them that there was no way we could go to Albania for at least six weeks. The chances of infection were too great and the medical conditions in Albania at that time were too primitive.

Of course, I was disappointed but God's timing is perfect. When I was released from the hospital we went back to the Houghton's to stay until I felt stronger. Charles Fritts and Herb went with me to get my motorhome and Herb drove it back for me. I had screws in my wrist and just below my elbow with two rods attached. I didn't feel up to driving yet.

Now I had to call my travel agent and reschedule our trip. I scheduled it for the middle of October. After about a month they removed the screws and put a regular cast on. The doctor didn't want me to go until the cast was off but I was determined. We left in October, cast and all. After a few more weeks I took my utility knife and cut the cast off myself.

By now the weather was getting cooler. I was so excited to show Sheila my beloved Albania.

After being up for twenty-four hours we finally landed in Tirana. We made the long walk from the plane to the airport. People inside were jammed in like sardines, pushing and talking loudly in a language we didn't know. We finally made it through customs, loaded our luggage on a cart and headed outside. This was the old airport. It was small and very primitive compared to what we were used to. As soon as we got outside we were bombarded by young children wanting money. It was a new experience for Sheila. They won't leave you alone. They follow you. We finally got a cab (if you want to call it that) and I told him as best I could where to go.

Once we arrived in town I had to point this way and that way. We arrived at Hervin's apartment building. It is a miracle that I could tell the driver how to get there! The roads were full of pot holes, water and mud.

Front of Glen & Sheila's
1st Apartment-3rd Floor
1994

I asked him if the apartment we had arranged to stay in was ready. He ran upstairs to the third floor and came back and said to give them thirty minutes. We paid the driver and left our luggage outside. We walked to the end of the road and sat down. Both of us were exhausted. While we waited, the people who lived in the apartment packed a few things and planned on staying with relatives. Finally, we were in the apartment. It was owned by a college professor named Rudi and his wife Tina. It had a small living/dining room with a very small kitchen off the dining area. There was a window in the kitchen that opened into the bathroom! It had one bedroom and a very small refrigerator in the hallway. The bathroom was full of plastic bottles to fill when the water came on. It had a sink, a turkish toilet and a shower head that sprayed the whole bathroom when you took your shower. This was the first time that Sheila ever seen a turkish toilet. Her first thought was, "Okay, time to go home."

The water came on once a day (hopefully) for an hour or so. It was usually in the afternoon so you tried to be home to fill up all the bottles and get your shower. The power was on in the morning and then off and then back on for supper and hopefully, throughout the evening.

The first Albanian that Sheila met was Hervin and she immediately fell in love with this young man. She loved his zeal for the Lord and the way he preached with such joy and enthusiasm. It was like having one of her children with her. Hervin spoke good English and the Lord put a love in Sheila's heart for this young believer that has only grown stronger over the years. To this day if you mention the name of Hervin Fushkati, Sheila will smile like a proud mama. He is like her "firstborn" in Albania but there would be others in the years to come.

****

One of the first things we did was go purchase some more Bibles. Highland Hills Church of God had a school at the time. A teacher there named Sandy Hovis had a school project where the students helped to raise money for the Bibles. She even had peel off stickers made that we could put in front of the Bibles. She was one of the first of a few that really encouraged us. Thank you, Sandy.

We immediately started giving out what we had brought. There was a couple of places I could take Sheila out to eat. The first place I took her was a hamburger joint sort of like (but not) McDonalds. We had to walk everywhere and after the first few days we noticed that Sheila had a blister on her heel the size of a quarter! I felt really bad about it but it didn't seem to bother her. It was about a four mile round trip wherever we went.

It seemed like a lot of traffic in Tirana but when we look back on the pictures there weren't that many vehicles. Today it is bumper to bumper and can be quite nerve wracking.

Sheila in front of Revolutionary Painting. One car in background-1994. (2004 street will be full cars.)

I was there when they installed the very first traffic light but the people didn't always pay attention to them. If they pulled up to a red light and nothing was coming they would go on through. This was the capital and you could see sheep on the street, horse drawn wagons right along with the vehicles. (The word car in Albania is offensive so that is why we try to use the word vehicle.)

Right down town Tirana. Wagon full of bottles.

Tirana has some historical statues and buildings but in those days the buildings were quite run down. Many of the government buildings had windows broken out. They were the same color that I have seen in other communist countries.

I took Sheila around and pointed out places of interest. There is a mosque right in the center of the city. You can hear the call to prayer at certain times. It always gives Sheila an eery feeling.

This was my third trip to Albania and each time I returned I could see improvements. The country was coming back to life after being in the cold dark winter of communism for so many years. Spring had returned to this tiny nation that had been shut off from the rest of the world for so long. It is like watching a newborn that changes so rapidly from day to day. Something new happening everyday! As I mentioned before there were small booths all along the road.

If one person was doing good then someone else would do the same thing. When I first came there the people didn't know what a banana was. When bananas came in people started selling bananas along the sidewalks.

The free market had opened up and people were doing whatever they could to earn a living. For decades they had been told what to do. Now they were on their own. It must have been a bit overwhelming but the people were happy to be free at last!

Man selling horma fruit
1994

The dictator, Enver Hoxha had kept the people paralyzed with fear. He had them convinced that Americans were making plans to bomb their country. You could see little concrete bunkers all over the country for the people to run to when the bombing began. Perhaps he believed this lie from satan himself. He must have been a very unhappy, paranoid human being.

Bomb Bunkers cover the landscape of Albania in 1994

There were very few tractors in the country at that time. In fact, I didn't see any. You mainly saw horse and wagons or even people carrying loads of hay or sticks on small donkeys or on their own heads. Even after seventeen years this is the way most of the people operate. Although, slowly people are bringing in more modern equipment. In the fall of 2009 we passed a shop in Durres that had tillers for sale. This was the first time we had seen this. The larger cities are becoming more modern.

Donkeys loaded down with hay.

You could see people all along the roads in small fields, leading their cows to graze in the fields. These weren't private owned fields. They belonged to the government. As I watched these people with their cows, God planted a desire in my heart to buy someone a milk cow. At this stage, it was just a thought...a small seed.

Mar 4:26-28 And he said, So is the kingdom of God, as if a man should cast seed into the ground; And should sleep, and rise night and day, and the seed should spring and grow up,

he knoweth not how. For the earth bringeth forth fruit of herself; first the blade, then the ear, after that the full corn in the ear.

People sitting all day with their cows.

****

We continued making friends with our neighbors and the people we would meet on our outings each day. Sheila and I were just lay people who had a heart for missions in general and Albania in particular. We didn't really know what we were doing. We just took it one day at a time and asked God to lead us and order our footsteps. The way God led me was to be friendly and give aid and assistance whenever I could. Mainly, He was leading me to just let the people know that I loved them and that more importantly, God loved them. I guess you could say I was sowing seeds of God's love and His "Word". Knowing that in the fulness of time God will give a great harvest of souls. This is always our main objective. To just let people know how much God loves them and cares about even their smallest desire.

****

Meanwhile, the church was beginning to grow and become established. We were now meeting in a room in a hotel. We met twice a week for worship. We hired a young man named Ermir to lead the singing. Hervin had approached me and said, "Look, if we don't hire Ermir to lead the worship then he will have to go to work in some bar because his father said he had to get a job." So I said, "Okay, we'll hire him." We agreed on a salary and I paid half and a man named Thomas paid the other half. Thomas was a German that the Church of God had sent in. Later on Ermir would become a pastor in the Church of God, and he and his wife "Vita" are two of our dearest friends. At this time he was still single.

Ermir leading worship in my apartment before he was ever hired.

Hervin was also having services on Saturday in a schoolyard in Vore. We got up early on Saturday morning and walked down to the train station which was two or three miles. When we got off the train in Vore we had to walk through a field and then across about a twelve inch water pipe that was crossing a big ditch. Sheila almost turned around at that point but with some coaxing she made it across. On the way back to the train we walked the long way around to avoid the pipe. By this time it was getting dark. During the day they played games with the children and then told them Bible stories and sang songs. The children loved it. At one point, some moslem men tried to intimidate us and make us stop our meeting but Hervin stood his ground.

November 8th, 1994 we were in Albania. Exactly, seven years earlier Sheila had started a forty day period of fasting and prayer for Albania and the suffering church in communist lands. She never dreamed when she began that fast that seven years later to the day that she would be standing in the land that had provoked that fast! If we had left when we originally planned then we would not have been there on this anniversary. That is what I meant when I said earlier that God's timing is perfect.

November 27th, 1994 we celebrated our 23rd wedding anniversary. We woke up that morning and the power was off. This wasn't too unusual. We walked down to our favorite restaurant that had only been open around a year. It is called "Stephen's Center" and is where all the missionaries gather. It was started and owned by an Albanian American and had food more like home. There was a Christian bookstore next door so we stopped in and Sheila bought a novel to read out loud to us because you couldn't understand most of what was on the television even when you did have power. So this was our entertainment. Sheila has always done this even when our kids were little. She would pop a big bowl of popcorn and then read out loud to all of us. Our daughter, Glenda still speaks fondly of those times.

When we got back to the apartment the power still wasn't on. Being the naïve Americans that we were and still are at times, Sheila said, "Oh, well it will be on in a few minutes." As it began to get dark we lit some candles. Sheila began reading the book to us by candle light. By bedtime the power still wasn't on and it was getting chilly in the apartment. Thank God Albanians have very heavy, warm blankets! The next morning the power still wasn't on! No problem...it would be coming on any minute. A few days later the power still wasn't on and our optimism wasn't quite as high but we still were expecting power any minute.

During this time, one day I went to a village with "Trouble" to share the gospel, give out some Bibles and make friends. We had to walk in to the village. We drove as far as we could and then walked the rest of the way. Sheila had asked me to bring home a loaf of bread but it was so late when we got back that I forgot. Sheila had the candles lit and was cooking some potatoes on a little burner that was fueled by a small bottle of propane gas like we would use to go camping. By now we were sort of adjusting to no power. With no power it meant no refrigeration. We found out that the cable to the apartments wasn't large enough to pull the load. When it was first installed all the people had was one or two light bulbs to burn but now they were using more electricity. Some had electric stoves. The power company was wanting some money. Hervin asked me to go to the meeting about the problem but I told him "No, this is an internal problem. It has nothing to do with me." About the time that we had resolved that we were going to be without power the rest of our stay, the power came back on! What we thought would be just a few hours had turned in to twelve days. At this time, in America that would never have been thought possible but our kids in Kentucky last year got a taste of what it is like, when the ice storm hit. Thank God for America and it's many blessings. May we never take our blessings and freedom for granted.

When we were there about a month, Sheila had a terrible attack of "homesickness". She asked me to change our tickets and take her home. I told her it would be too expensive. She always jokes that when I wanted to come home early it was "possible" but when she wanted to it was "impossible". After a day or so she was feeling better. We both stayed well the whole trip. God has always kept us from any kind of serious sickness. Thank you, Jesus!

December 19th arrived and it was time to return to the states. We both were pleased with our trip and any encouragement we had been able to give. We were looking forward to being home but as we rode to the airport, in my mind I was already planning my next trip. On our way home we stopped in Rome and spent a couple of days. I had been there before but it was Sheila's first time and I wanted to show her some of the historical sites. I think she was more excited to see a bathtub and a western toilet!

April picked us up at the Knoxville airport. It was a joyful reunion, especially between mother and daughter. It was good to be in our own bed that night. I fell asleep thinking about the people I had left behind and praying for the young believers and the new little church.

Chapter 3

1995-2001

The Sower Soweth the Word

After we returned we took the motorhome to Florida and spent a few months. Everyone I met had to listen to me talk about Albania. When we returned to Tennessee I rented a spot at the "Cross-eyed Cricket" campground. Sheila got a job working for an answering service. She had no intention of returning at this time. The culture shock was a bit too much for her.

I returned to Albania in April and planned on staying for two months. After a month without Sheila by my side I changed my ticket and came home early. This is why she teases me because I had told her it wasn't possible when she wanted to come home.

I stayed in Rudi's apartment again. I deposited money in Hervin's account for salary. After a few days he met with me and said that the

Church of God under Paul Lauster and Thomas (the man from Germany) was taking over the finances. I said, “Okay”. I asked for the bank book so that I could withdraw the funds that I had deposited. I didn’t want there to be any confusion and both of us to be paying the salaries. No one from headquarters had made contact with me to let me know what was going on. I have to be honest and admit that this hurt me but I rolled it over on God and knew He had something else for me to do. The little church was doing good and that was the main thing.

I continued doing what I knew to do, giving out aid and Bibles, making friends and sowing the Word and “ seeds of love”.

Back in the states at the end of summer Sheila and I went to a Church of God missions conference in south Florida. Once again, the different missions speakers inspired us to keep going. Paul Lauster was there and we talked. There had been some accusations made about me on my last trip concerning a girl. I had told this person to bring the accuser to me so that I could confront him face to face but the person never did. Paul asked me if I had told Sheila (who was sitting with us) and I told him “yes”. He seemed happy that everything was straightened out. Years later one of the men came to me and apologized. In fact, he apologized more than once (four different occasions). It was just that old enemy, “satan” the accuser of the brethren trying to stop God’s plans. Guess what? He lost again!

When we returned to Tennessee I received a call that our son Glen Jr. wasn’t doing too good in Florida. He was running with the wrong crowd. He had stopped going to church and his sister Glenda was concerned about him. I hung up the phone and talked to Sheila. We called Glen Jr. and told him we thought he needed to come home. I told him I would help him get started in the building business. He said, “Okay”. Sheila and I went out and bought a lot. Within a few days our son walked through the door. We were so glad to have him home even if we were living in a motorhome. Sheila was working for another company now that was closer to home. She would help us on her days off. By Thanksgiving we had our first house ready to paint. So Sheila, Glen Jr. and I painted all morning. We wore our paint splattered clothes to Shoney's for our Thanksgiving dinner. Then went back and finished painting. I planned on leaving after Christmas to spend some time in Florida and I wanted to get this first house finished. One day at work Sheila was looking in the newspaper and saw an ad for two lots for $7000. That seemed unreal so we called and got directions. We had never been out in this area. It is called "Lake Awana". Sure enough there were two nice flat lots that were side by side. We bought them immediately and I told Glen Jr. to pick out which lot he wanted. I would take the other one. We started our second house which would be Glen Jrs.' before I left for Florida.

I planned to return to Albania in the fall of 1996.

1996 (Year of Tragedy)

In January we drove to Florida to spend a few months. On Valentines Day we received a call from our daughter "April" in Tennessee that she was expecting her first child. She was so happy. April always loved babies and small children. She can see humor in everything they do and actually make it funnier when she tells you what they have said or done.

Glen Jr. was staying with her while we were in Florida. Everything was going good.

When we returned we began working vigorously on Jrs.' house and started one next door for us. We planned on renting it to April. We felt like they could watch out for each other when we were out of town. By the end of May we had both houses finished and another one started in the same neighborhood. Glen Jr. had been in his about a month. We now helped April and her husband move in to the one next door. We got everything moved and planned on leaving the next day for a short vacation to Florida. April and Glen Jr. came with us. We had a fun trip driving down enjoying both of our kids. We parked the motorhome at Sheila's mother's for a few days. Glen Jr. went to spend time with his cousins. April stayed with her grandma. After a day or so we took April with us to Daytona Beach for a few days. By now she was showing and her baby was moving all the time. She enjoyed her time off from work and loved walking on the beach spending time with her mom. She already had her baby named and had a seashell spray painted with Sierra's name on it along with her's and Shawn's. Glen Jr. celebrated his 24th birthday while we were at the beach. We were sorry that we weren't with him. After a week or so we returned home. April had to be back to work. Glen Jr. planned on leaving the next day. He was going to drive back his brother Jerry's car. Jerry and his wife had just moved back to Tennessee. We had only been home a short while and I went down the block to see my neighbor. While I was there, April came over (we were parked next to April) and said she was bleeding. Sheila went with April and Shawn to the hospital. They immediately put April in a room and tried to stop her labor. It was Sunday afternoon when she went to the hospital and in the early hours of the morning on Tuesday, June 11th our little Sierra was born. She weighed fifteen ounces and you could hold her in your hand. I wasn't there (Glen Jr. and I had been there earlier in the evening) but Sheila said the family members that were there were standing around April's bed. Each one held Sierra for a moment and then they handed her to April. (The first thing that April usually does when she sees a newborn is look at their feet.) April was shaking but not crying. She looked at her and stroked her hair, held her little hands and then slowly pulled back the small blanket and looked at her tiny feet. When she saw Sierra's feet that had been kicking her so vigorously a few days before she burst into tears. To this day, Sheila weeps when she recalls this scene. Sheila had become very bonded to Sierra while she was in the womb. Now her heart was breaking for her own loss and the loss of her daughter. As soon as Sheila called April's sister "Glenda", she made plans to drive up and be with her sister. Glenda is always there when you need her. She arrived the next day. We had Sierra's funeral on Thursday afternoon. She was buried in her father's family plot in Morristown.

Glenda stayed with April until Sunday morning June 16th. On her way out she stopped to say good-bye to Glen Jr. It was Father's Day. After the church service Sheila took me out for Father's Day and Glen Jr. out for his birthday that we had missed. Then she took him to Sears and bought him a tool he had been wanting. It was called a Sawzall. He needed it to cut the holes for the air conditioning ducts. He had been using a skill saw but this would be easier. Jr. was really pleased. The next day he showed his mom the holes and told her how much easier it had been.

Wednesday, June 19th Sheila's mother "Rene" and sister-in-law "Cindy" came to spend a few days with April and try to cheer her up.

Thursday, June 20th Sheila, her mom and Glen Jr. (her mom's first grandchild) went to Knoxville to pick up some material. On the way back they stopped and enjoyed a meal and a time of fellowship at Cracker Barrel . Meanwhile, in Florida Rene's prayer partner kept hearing the Lord say, "Pray for Rene". When they got back to Lake Awana, Sheila dropped Glen Jr. off at the job and then took her mom to April's. April had some trash to burn so Sheila took it to the jobsite and put it on the trash they were about to burn. There was a little “Vols” bear in the bag that played “Rocky Top”. Sheila and Jr. were in the house and Sheila was looking out the window watching the fire when she heard “Rocky Top” start playing. She said, “Oh, look at the little Vols bear burning. It’s playing Rocky Top and looks so sad.” Jr. rushed to the window to look and got a sorrowful look on his face. He said sadly, “Why did ya’ll throw him away?” Jr. had such a tender heart that he could feel compassion even for a toy bear.

When Jr. and I finished working that day, Glen Jr. went home and took a shower. His mom fixed him a sandwich. I was in the shower. He ate his sandwich, gave his mother and grandmother a kiss and said he would see them tomorrow.

Friday, June 21st at 3:10 a.m. the phone rang. Sheila answered it and someone asked to speak to Glen Watson. She handed the phone to me. The person on the phone told me that my son had been in an accident and was at the Loudon Hospital. Sheila and I quickly dressed. We couldn't take her mother with us because we only had a small truck. We thought we would need the room to bring Glen Jr. home in. When we arrived at the hospital, instead of taking us to Glen Jr. they took us to a small room. The doctor came in and told us our son had not survived the accident. We were stunned. We both began to weep. Sheila's nose started bleeding! I went back to identify the body. He was still warm. We called our spiritual parents, Barb and Herb. They arrived a short time later with our pastor, Charles Fritts. What would we do without Jesus and the Body of Christ? We buried April's firstborn the week before, now we would bury Sheila's firstborn! Glenda who had only been home a few days would be making the trip again to bury her baby brother. There was something to be thankful for during this time. Sheila's mother was already here. She had got to spend time with Glen Jr. one last time and she didn't have to make that trip after just learning of his death. For that we will always be thankful and take comfort in knowing that none of this took God by surprise. We both had perfect peace that our son was with the Lord. It was extremely difficult to finish that house that we had started together. To go there without Glen Jr. was almost unbearable. Glenda's husband John helped me with the Heating and Air unit before he left. That was who taught Glen Jr. about it. We somehow made it through those dark days and finished the house. By now it was September and I decided I may as well follow through with my plans to return to Albania. I don't have many memories of that trip (maybe because I was still grieving). I can't even find any pictures but I know that I continued doing what I had been doing. Giving out aid, love and encouragement.

I do remember giving a young preacher some dress clothes that I had bought a few years earlier for Glen Jr. to wear to church. When I gave them to him he said, "I was wondering what I was going to wear Sunday to preach my first sermon." They fit him perfect. A couple of years later this young man's mother was accidentally shot while cooking supper on her balcony. He told me there were about 32 apartments tied together in his building and that when they were built no one was a

Christian and now all of them are Christians. Praise the Lord!

1997 (Country In Chaos)

When I returned to Albania in the spring of '97 the country was in chaos due to a corrupt failed pyramid scheme that robbed hundreds of thousands of Albanians of their life savings. I had my suitcases loaded once again with aid and I had quite a bit of cash in my carry on luggage. I had no knowledge of this crisis when I left the states. I just knew God was calling me to Albania. When I arrived at the airport the security put me in a room and strip searched me. I got a cab and before we got three or four miles down the road our cab was stopped by armed men with black hoods over their faces. They wanted to look through my luggage and I said, "No!" (It must have been the boldness of the Lord because they didn't argue with me.) Then they asked to see my passport. I let them see my passport and then they waved me on through. When we got out of their sight my driver started laughing. I think he was surprised at my boldness but he knew I had done the right thing.

When I got to Rudi's apartment I took some clothing out of my suitcase and gave it to Rudi. Rudi told me not to go up town. To stay close to the apartment. I did stay out of the center but I walked around the edges. One day as I was walking I saw a man with a hood stopping traffic and checking the vehicles. One truck sped past me and the hooded man drew his gun and shouted at the truck. The truck came to a stop and the armed man ran up to him and started shouting at him. They were arguing back and forth but he finally let him go. After a week or less my Albanian friends urged me to go home. They were afraid something might happen to me. I left with a heavy heart and promised that I would return.

1998 NEW LIFE

When I returned in '97 I didn't know what to do with myself. The day before my son's accident we had carried a temporary power pole across the street to a new lot we had bought. Not knowing what to do I turned to what I knew. I went across the street and started laying out a new house. I got it started and then we went to Florida for a few months. While we were down there we found out that April was expecting another child.

In April, we began to build with all our energy. It wasn't as easy without the help of "Junebug". Nevertheless, by July we were moved out of the motorhome and in to a real house again. We had lived in the motorhome for over four years. It was nice to stretch out a little. On August 4th God blessed us beyond measure with another granddaughter "Destiny Jade". God has used this little girl to bring so much joy and healing to us.

In September I returned to Albania. Once again, I cut my trip short. After I did what I felt I was supposed to do I was anxious to get back home. Albania was still healing from the chaos of the 1997 Civil War. I saw some improvements but everything was moving slowly.

1999 Kosavar Crisis

As usual, we went to Florida the winter of 1999. When we returned to Tennessee we started attending New Vision where Rick and Lisa Lambert were pastors. I prepared to go back to Albania. I told Sheila if it was me I would like something new with a tag still on it. Goody's clothing store was having a sale so Sheila and I went and bought brand new dresses and men's shirts.

The Kosavar refugee crisis was going on. Thousands of Albanians fled from Kosova because they were being slaughtered by the Serbs. There were about 21 refugees living in an apartment above me. A lady that lived in our building would go around trying to get food, clothing, money etc… to help them. I gave most of the new clothing to her for the refugees. She is a very kind woman. When Sheila and I first stayed in this building her teenage daughter would visit us. I was at her wedding. Her son "Ilir" played the drums for our church. We went to visit this lady in 2003 and were saddened to hear that this daughter had died leaving behind two small children. We still miss her, but we will see her in Heaven.

****

When I got back home I began encouraging Rick and Lisa to go with me to Albania. Sheila still had not returned to Albania. Rick and Lisa had never been to Israel so we decided to take a little less than a week in Albania and then take a trip to Israel. It had been five years since Sheila had been in Albania. She was pleasantly surprised to see the improvements in the airport and the runway. They had built a new airport even though it was small it was much nicer. Also, there was a new road from the airport. When we arrived at Rudi's there were even more surprises. The bathroom was completely remodeled! It had an enclosed shower, a western toilet and even a bidet! Rudi was proudly showing it to Sheila and trying to explain what the bidet was for. Rudi doesn't speak English and so he showed her she could wash her feet in it. Rudi is a devout muslim. His wife Tina was an atheist. We gave them Bibles and tried to witness but I don't know if they have ever changed. We tried to visit them on our last trip in 2009 but they weren't home. We left them a little booklet. When you pray remember this dear couple.

I had hoped to introduce Rick and Lisa to Hervin but he was being trained by the Church of God in Germany and would be gone for a few years. The church kind of went down at that time but they were training him to be the Overseer for Albania.

Even though we only had about week there Rick and Lisa were so excited to finally be on a missions trip. Missions has always been in Lisa's heart. They had loaded their suitcases with socks, toys, tylenol samples, etc. As soon as we got in the apartment they bagged up some stuff and went around the neighborhood giving items out (especially to the children). Something kind of humorous that happened....they had brought a bunch of toy yo-yos. They were a big hit and ran out of them. There were still some kids that wanted one so Lisa was going from shop to shop and asking, "Yo-yo? Yo-yo?" They just looked at her like she was nuts. In Albania the word "yo" means "no" so it sounded to them like she was asking, "No, no? No, no?" We laughed and finally gave up on the yo-yos. We rented a car and driver one day and he took us to Elbasan which is a beautiful drive and then over to Durres. In Durres we took them to see the Coliseum which is like the one in Rome on a smaller scale. The Albanians discovered it not that many years ago by accident. They were drilling a well for a house (I think) and the bit fell off in a hole. When they investigated they discovered that under this area that had been covered over was the Coliseum. They say that Titus was murdered there. You can see where they kept the wild animals and also where there is evidence that Christians had been down there. The Albanians say that it is older than the one in Rome. It was built by the Romans.

Coliseum - Durres, Albania (1999)
Glen & Rick Lambert

It was a good first trip for Rick and Lisa.

2000 – Weary in Well Doing

In 2000 Sheila was invited to go with Jean Mabry and a large group of homeschoolers to Israel. The children ranged in ages from teenagers to a two year old. They were dancers and were going to dance all over Israel and pray for the land. As Sheila made plans for Israel I began making plans to return to Albania. We would fly together as far as Amsterdam and then split up. We would meet back up in Amsterdam in a couple of weeks.

One day while we were still in Florida and staying at the RV Park in Clermont, Sheila and I went out to eat and when we drove back in to the park I saw a man and woman with their trunk lid open. Curious....I stopped and asked them what they were selling. They had a trunk full of nice, thick t-shirts made for the GAP retail stores. They had brought them down from North Carolina to bring them to a woman that was going to sell them at a huge flea market. The woman got sick and couldn't do it so they were going to try to sell them from their car. I told them that I might be interested in buying them if the price was right because I wanted to take them to give away in Albania. It turned out that they were Christians and the man told his wife to make me a good deal. She said she would let me have them all for two hundred dollars. There was over three hundred shirts that sold retail for $5.99! I was so thrilled. I loaded the back of my motorhome with them. It was really loaded down. Meanwhile, we got to talking and found out we had some things in common. This couple (they were old enough to be Sheila's parents) had a son and a daughter just like Sheila and I. Their kids were in college and had come home for a holiday. On their way back to school they were both killed in an auto accident! Their story was even more heartbreaking than ours. At least we still had our other children. Not only that, their daughter's name was Sheila! After we had loaded the motorhome with the shirts and gave her a check for $200, a few minutes later she came back and gave us $50, plus a t-shirt for Sheila and a book that Sheila had been wanting called the Prayer of Jabez! Only the Lord knew she wanted that book. This couple was such a blessing to us and I pray that God blesses them many times over.

When I returned it was the beginning of August and very hot and muggy in Tirana. My suitcases were so full that I had to tie them together. I only had a short time so I immediately began sowing seeds of love by giving out Bibles, medicine, clothing, Gap t-shirts and lots of hugs.

Gap T-Shirts. It took three trips to give them all away! God is our provider!

One night while I was trying to rest in my hot, stuffy room I dozed off and was awakened by something biting my leg. I reached out in the darkness and slapped whatever it was off my leg. I turned on the light and there was a large, dark bug about two or three inches long. It had been chewing on my leg. I don't know what it was but it left a sore on my leg. It took three or four weeks for it to heal.

The heat on this trip had been stifling and I was glad to get on the air-conditioned plane. As I lay my head back on my seat, I closed my eyes and thought to myself, "I'm getting too old for this. I think this was my last trip." I was tired and feeling a little down. However, I didn't say anything to Sheila. I kept it to myself for the time being but God knew how I felt and that I was needing some encouragement.

In the fall Sheila and I headed back to Florida. Not long after we got there Sheila had an opportunity to work a couple of days for her cousin. She made a hundred dollars. The Lord spoke to her and told her to give half of it for Albania. She came home, took an empty coffee creamer jar and wrote "Albania" on the outside. She put the fifty dollars in it and brought it to me and said, “This is for your next trip to Albania.” I still didn’t tell her what I had been thinking about not returning. She got to work the next week and the Lord told her to do the same thing. Then our daughter “April” who was living in Florida at the time, received some money and she felt impressed to put part of it in the jar! I began to get excited and started putting money in it also. I realized that God wasn’t through with me. I would be going back again. I praise God that He sent me encouragement when I needed it. His timing is perfect!

2001 – Renewed Hope

Back in Tennessee, my hope and strength renewed, I started preparing for my next trip.

We had been renting Glen Jr.’s home to a young couple named Angie and Dean. When they first rented the house they weren’t saved. They were having hard financial times but Angie began giving me bags of clothing that she gathered up for Albania. As she did this, their financial situation began to improve. Then Dean went to a revival and got "born again"! Angie and the kids followed. They became involved in church and God began to bless them so much that they were able to buy their own home! I believe it all started with the small seed that Angie sowed to Albania. When they moved out we fixed the home up for our daughter who was moving back near the end of August. We were happy to have her back home and across the street from us. Sheila would have some company when I made my next trip.

I was happy and excited about returning to Albania. On September 7, 2001 I flew from Knoxville to Washington, D.C. never dreaming what would be taking place just four days later. I arrived on Saturday, got a room and bought some water and food. Sunday I went to church and then rested from the trip. Monday and Tuesday I went to visit different friends and take them some medicine and clothing. They are always so happy to see us. It means so much to them to know that they aren't forgotten, that I really care about them. Wednesday morning my translator and driver arrived to take me to

Elbasan. This was when I first heard about 911. My translator asked me if I was still going to go to Elbasan. I said, "Yes. We already have everything packed and ready to give out. I'll check on the situation when I get back." All along the way to Elbasan, if I saw someone that I felt impressed to bless I would have the driver pull over. We gave out Bibles, toys, Gap t-shirts, other clothes and shoes. We were gone all day and got back to Tirana late in the afternoon. I think the driver and translator were surprised that I wasn't all shook up about what was going on in the states. I had perfect peace. I had told Sheila before I left that if I didn't see her again on this side I would see her on "the other side". We both had peace. Sheila kept getting phone calls from anxious relatives wanting know if she had heard from me. She told them, "No, not yet but I have peace."

The next day I went to the "Stephen Center" restaurant to find out what was happening. There were some missionaries that had been there awhile and they were trying to get tickets to go home. Anxious families in the states were wanting some of them to come home. Some had heard they could get tickets on Swiss Air but that turned out to be a rumor. No one could get tickets because no one was flying in at that time to the states. You could feel the tension and anxiety in the air. The enemy was trying to use fear to stop the work of God. I wasn't anxious. I had a return ticket but it wasn't due to fly out for nineteen more days. I figured everything would be calmed down by then and Praise the Lord, it was! I finally got a call through to Sheila to let her know that I was fine. I had to make my calls in a semi-trailer that had phones. That was my only means of communication at the time. Email wasn't as common there as it is now. I always called Sheila on Mondays around noon which is six in the morning in the states.

The Albanians all expressed their sympathies to me for what had happened in America. They could relate to sorrow and tragedy on a national level more than most Americans because they have been invaded so many times in their history.

I returned to the states without any problems. Once again God had been faithful to me and encouraged me to keep going.

Chapter 4

2002

The Heavens Begin to Open Up!

In the beginning of 2002 we were back at the RV Park in Clermont, Florida. One day we were watching James Robison's program and he had a couple on from Albania. It was David and Valbona Pennoyer. David was a pastor from Canada that God led to Albania. While he was there he met his wife who is an Albanian. They have a church in Durres. I was planning a trip in the spring and Sheila asked me to check out this church. So while I was in Tirana on my spring trip I went over to Durres one Sunday and met David. We felt that God was leading us to a new city even though we felt comfortable in Tirana. I got David's email so we could stay in touch. At some point during this time Sheila said, "If you really feel called to Albania then why don't we go and stay for a year?" So we began praying about that. To me it was like saying "sic em" to a dog.

People began asking me what the name of my ministry was. I didn't have a name but one Saturday night in August, Sheila couldn't sleep. She got up and was praying for Albania. She kept hearing a little chorus that we used to sing..."Arise shine for thy light has come, arise shine for thy light has come. And the glory of the Lord has risen, and the glory of the Lord has come and the glory of the Lord has risen upon thee." Over and over she heard it. It was like a light came on. She told me later that she thought the name of our ministry was supposed to be "Arise Shine Albanian Ministry". That is how we got our name. God also that same night gave her a vision for the church that we attend in the states. So far that vision hasn't come to pass but we won't be surprised when it does.

We planned to take a three week trip to Durres in September. We had decided to take the leap of faith and leave our family for a year in 2003. We were taking this short trip to make some plans and do what we had been doing for ten years. Rick and Lisa went with us again. We had been in contact with David Pennoyer and planned on staying in his facility. Rick and Lisa could only stay for a week. Rick was going to preach that Sunday but he had an attack of kidney stones and so Lisa had to preach. The day that Rick and Lisa left Sheila was in bed with a bad headache so we didn't get to go with them to the airport. We stayed quite busy during our stay. In fact, we were helping serve lunch to the children of the feeding program right up until they took us to the airport. While we were there we met a couple from Vermont. They were there full time and were retired dairy farmers. There names are Brent and Carol. They took us to look at some apartments but we didn't make any final decisions at that time.

We went to a Perry Stone Campmeeting when we got back home. We were all hyped up about Albania. We went out to eat with some friends that we see there every year……Ben, Pauline, Bobbie and Tommy. While we were fellowshiping I shared with them about my desire to someday buy a poor family a milk cow before I made my final trip to Albania. Ben and Pauline are leaders in their church. Both of them are Sunday school teachers. Ben caught the vision. He said he was going to tell his church about the milk cow. God was up to something! Something good!

****

2003 – Showers of Blessings!

At the beginning of the year we once again went to Florida for a month. We cut our trip short because we had much to do before we left for Albania. We were leaving on April 22, 2003. One day while we were in Florida we received a phone call from our friend, Barb Houghton. She said that she had received a letter from Ben. She didn't pay attention to whom it was addressed and opened it. When she opened it there were several checks in it made out to me for a milk cow in Albania. At the time, I thought a cow would probably be about $300. This turned out not to be the case. I was so excited to see how other people were getting involved in the mission!

One Sunday we went to the Church of God in Clermont and I started a conversation with a man that was on the missions board in

Cleveland. He told me to make a call to King's Pharmaceuticals when I got home and they would give me a drop. Sheila and I expected a small box of supplies. When we received the "drop" it was two large boxes! They were filled with off brand tylenol, ibuprofen, baby lotion, arthritis creams, hydrocortizone cream, baby powder and I can't remember what else! It was almost $2,000.00 worth of supplies! I also, went to the Sock Factory in Sweetwater to buy some socks. I always went there to buy socks. When I went in there this time I told him I wanted to buy a hundred dollars worth of socks. Sheila said don't get too many because we had to pack extra for ourselves because we were going to be gone for a year. The girls asked could I use these socks that had a stitch or two in the wrong place. I said, "Yes!" They started bagging up so many socks that I thought maybe they had misunderstood me so I laid down a hundred dollars in different bills. The owner pick up half the money and put it back in my pocket and said come go with me. We went to the back and he said, "You grab those two boxes and I'll grab these two." I was in my corvette and I had to put the top down to get all of the socks in! I drove away with such joy at how God was supplying exceeding, abundantly above what I could ask or think! We had so many socks and supplies from the pharmaceutical company that we had to pay for an extra four pieces of luggage to the airline. We took the socks and other supplies to Barb and Herb's basement. Herb helped me to take the supplies out of the boxes so that we would have more room. David Pennoyer had asked us to bring over some equipment to show the God Story video, so that took up some of our space.

We put our house up for sale and prayed that it would sell before we had to leave. God heard our prayers and we began moving our furniture across the street in to a small storage trailer. We must have been a sight to our neighbors. We didn't have a truck and so Sheila and I were moving things over in a wheel-barrow. We even moved our large mattress on it. We started joking and laughing and I said, "Maybe we should start a moving company." We moved in to the motorhome and parked it across the street on our rental property. We still did not have our money from the house. We had a few days before we left and we worked feverishly to get the final few items completed before we could close. We closed the day before we left! Talk about "down to the wire"! Sheila donated her share of the profit from the house to the Albanian ministry. I know God will multiply it back to her and to all of us that have given so generously. God keeps good records and He loves to see his children step out in faith and trust Him. Barb was so excited about the cows that she decided she wanted to donate one, too! Before we left we had enough money to buy four cows! Praise the Lord, God was giving me my heart's desire.

We were at the laundromat one day before we left because we no longer had a washer and dryer. I started talking about Albania to a lady named Carol Holt. It turned out that she also attended the "Church of God". I told her about Sheila putting money in a creamer jar. She gave me ten dollars before I left and said she was going to get her a creamer jar. Everywhere I went it seemed that people wanted to help. I can't name them all but you know who you are and I pray God's blessing on you.

During this time of preparation, Sheila was also preparing her heart to leave April and Destiny. The bond between Sheila and her granddaughter is so strong. By now Destiny was four years old and loved being with Granny. She always said, "I'm Granny's girl" and she still says it. She begged her granny not to go. Sheila told her that there were people that might go to hell if she didn't go. Not really understanding she said, "I don't care. Let them go to hell." I guess in her mind it was like going to the Walmart. Once again, leaving her girls was the most difficult part of going for Sheila. She had to spend much time in prayer and the Word to silence the voice of the enemy. She would miss seeing Destiny start her first year of school, her first experiece in cheerleading, etc., but since we first met, Sheila's first love has always been Jesus. This love is what gave her the courage to obey God and I praise the Lord for it.

Destiny and April come over to say good-bye to "Granny" and "Pappy"

A couple of days before we left we bought our first digital camera. We didn't know anything about them. We were just learning about sending emails and we wanted to be able to attach pictures so friends and family could see what we were doing. We also bought a DVD player so that we could show the God Story video. Sheila realized she needed something for the camera so we got back in the car and headed back to Walmart. As we were getting on to the interstate we saw a brand new sling for a broken arm. We stopped to pick it up thinking we would probably need it in Albania or else God wouldn't have had it on the side of the road. We were only in Albania a few days when we went to visit a family with Brent and Carol (the missionaries from Vermont). Lying on the bed was a young man with a broken arm! Of course, we gave him the sling.

Navy blue sling lying on the boy. God sees and cares about the smallest need.

April 22 had finally arrived. We hadn't slept very good the night before. We seldom do. Barb and Herb took us to the airport and our neighbor "Joe" took our luggage in his pick up truck. We had eight suitcases stuffed full and our carry on luggage. At that time you could put seventy pounds in your checked luggage. Now you can only put fifty pounds. We made use of every pound! We were off on our great adventure with God not knowing what He would do but we knew it would be good whatever it was! We were not disappointed.

We arrived in Tirana on April 23rd and were picked up by Brent in the church van from David Pennoyer's church. When we got to the church (which has a floor for missionaries) we unloaded our luggage and immediately went in to the church which was in the middle of a service. We were exhausted but didn't want to disappoint the people. When we walked in they all started clapping for us! They made us feel so welcome.

Chapter 5

Visions Begin to Come to Pass

We stayed in the church facility for about a week while we looked at different apartments. The main thing Sheila prayed for was an apartment with a bathtub. One day we had laid down to rest in the afternoon. When Sheila got up she came back to the room and said, "Glen, there is a small child asleep in the other room!" I got up and sure enough there was what looked like a toddler sound asleep on the bed! He really was about three. We didn't know what to think. We didn't dare leave him to go get something to eat. When he woke up, his pants were wet but we didn't have anything to change him in. Sheila brought him to the table and gave him a snack. We couldn't communicate with him because he spoke Albanian! Finally, there was a knock at the door. His parents, Ilir and Blerta came in. They worked for the church and had gone to a meeting in another village! This was our first time that we remember meeting "Joshua". We kept thinking, "What if Sheila hadn't looked in the spare room and we had left?" He could have turned on the gas stove! We would come to love this family very much and to work in the ministry with them. It turned out that they would leave Joshua at their apartment many times during nap time. When we finally decided on an apartment (which had a bathtub) it was right next door to this young couple. Once again, God was up to something good. Blerta could speak good English and whenever we had a question, we could go out to our courtyard and yell up to Blerta's apartment. She lived on the top floor of a building with three other apartments. She would come running out on her balcony and look down into our yard and help us in any way she could. She and Ilir helped to fill the empty place in our hearts that we felt for the kids we left in the states. Thank you Jesus for this couple that has a heart for You! We miss them when we are in the states just like we miss our kids when we are in Albania.

Blerta leading praise and worship at a village meeting. Ilir was playing the guitar.

Once we got settled, I began in earnest to look for a milk cow. We had found the family that we wanted to give the first cow to. Brent helped us and we finally found a cow. We called the first cow "Josephine". Named after the man that purchased it. We got in the church van and Brent drove us as far as we could and then we got out to walk. It was a sunny but still cool, windy day. When we got to where the cow was we looked her over. Brent was a former dairy farmer and I also grew up on a dairy farm. She looked like a good cow. We were surprised to find out that a good cow cost between $800-$1200! We paid the money and then the woman that owned the cow had to walk it to the new owner. Brent and the others went in the van but I walked with the owner and it is a long walk!

Our first cow and the family we bought it from.

We finally arrived at the new owners house. Their names are Dila and Peter. When we got there we saw an invalid child lying on the ground. His name is Koli. He is the oldest of four children. When we gave Dila the cow she started crying, another lady that was with us started crying, too! We all got choked up. Dila told us that she had always dreamed of owning a cow but never thought she would. Dila is a Christian and attends David's church. We took Blerta with us a couple of weeks later to see how everything was going with the cow. Dila told us through the translator that since receiving the cow that her health was returning and that she was happy like the day one of her children were born! Thank you, Jesus!

Glen, "Josephine", Dila and her two sons. The one in the cradle is 2. He would lie there without complaint twice a day for two hours! They think it makes his back grow straight. I've seen this a few times. I don't think an American toddler would lie there like that! I know ours wouldn't!

****

God is our father and just like earthly parents he cares about our smallest desires. He demonstrated this to us the second Sunday that we were in Albania. We had just moved in to our own apartment. After church, Sheila and I walked to a restaurant a few blocks from the church. For some reason while we were eating Sheila began thinking about maple syrup. She lamented, "Oh, I wish I had brought that little bottle of syrup from the Cracker Barrel." That is all she said. We finished our meal and walked home. Several hours later there was a knock on our door. It was our friends from Vermont, Brent and Carol. One thing they do when they are home is make maple syrup. Carol had what looked like a quart jug of maple syrup with her. She said she brought us a welcome gift! What a gift it was. To part with one of her jugs of syrup to us was a great sacrifice. Even more, to see how God gave Sheila her desire.....above and beyond what she wanted made us feel pretty special in God's eyes. We will never forget how God used this couple to encourage us that day. Thank you, Brent and Carol.

Brent and Carol on far right of picture.

When we shared this story in an email. Someone wrote back and said, "Wow. What if she had wished for a "Cracker Barrel! Wonder what she would have got?" We laughed. We were having such a good time. It seemed like almost everyday was a joy.

****

Not long after we arrived we were pleasantly surprised to receive a visit from Hervin (Sheila's first "son" in Albania). He was finally back in Albania and was the overseer for the COG in Albania. It had been nine years since Sheila had seen him. What a joy to see what God was doing in this young man's life.

Chapter 6

Emails

Saturday, May 3, 2003

Hello everyone,

Glen was up bright and early this morning to go look for some milk cows. They don't have a cattle auction here like they do in the states so it is going to be interesting to see where he gets these milk cows from.

God did some more neat things for us yesterday. I said that I needed some cups, dinner plates, a towel bar for the bathroom, some tupperware for leftovers, and we wanted a couple of chairs for outside and we needed a gas heater for this winter. Well, yesterday a missionary that is returning to the states had a giveaway! We were given china (including dinner plates, sandwich plates, cups, saucers, a serving platter, and a large serving bowl, tupperware, "two towel bars and soap dishes!", plus they had two chairs and a gas heater they sold at a reasonable price! Not only that but they gave us Albanian Bibles, New Testaments, and other spiritual books in Albanian for us to take to the villages! God is so good!

Friday, May 16, 2003

Hello world (all twenty of you) out there in cyber space. Well, I had quite an exciting day this past Tuesday. It was the first time I ever saw someone milk a cow! After the ladies' Bible study, the young woman that we gave the second cow to came to the church and said she was having problems milking the cow. Well, Brent and Glen said they would go and check the cow for sickness and milk the cow. They brought Carol and me along. We also had another big man with us named Ben. He is an Albanian vetinarian. Being a "City Girl" this was a new experience for me but I "think" I know how it is done now. They pushed the cow up next to the building, Glen held the cow by the horns, the lady sat down with a bucket under the cow, and Brent pulled the cow's tail up! Now, I was staying back a distance but I believe

(I could be mistaken) but what it looked like to me was when Brent pulled up the cow's tail the milk came out! I think the harder you pull the tail the more milk you get! (Think about the sacrifice of the poor cow the next time you pour milk on your cereal). This "City Girl" has come a long way since Glen and I planted our first three tomato plants over thirty years ago. Boy, was I dumb back then! Can you believe I thought you get one tomato per plant and that it grew under the ground? And now look at me, I can tell you like a pro how to milk a cow! I have to admit that I'm a bit concerned for the little gal who has to milk the cow everyday. Who is going to hold it by the horns and yank the tail while she holds the bucket? Let me know if you have any ideas. I'm attaching some pictures of the whole procedure for you to see.

P.S. Glen said to tell John, Stan and Jarvis that he needs them to come help him castrate some bulls. He tried it the other day by himself! Sorry, but I don't have a picture of that. Glen and the bull were moving too fast!! Ha! Ha!

P.P.S. Seriously, the pictures are of the second cow we bought and it is a young cow that had never been milked and was missing her calf. Glen and Brent got her calmed down and we haven't heard anymore from the girl so we assume everything is going okay now. The other picture I attached is of people drawing water from a well. They have a wire attached to a coke bottle and lower it down into the well. It takes quite a while to fill one of their containers this way. Some of them have to walk about two miles, pushing a wheel barrow with three or four containers.

Sheila watches at a distance while they milk the 2nd milk cow.

Children drawing water with plastic bottle.

****

Monday, May 19, 2003

The people that received the third milk cow have two handicapped children (both boys). They have two girls that are normal. It was very sad when we arrived to see these children. Especially, the oldest. He was lying on a blanket on a concrete front porch. He was so small. He looked like about a three year old but I think he was six or seven. I don't know what is wrong with him. The other baby boy has Downs Syndrome. He was lying in a cradle. This family was so grateful to receive a cow.

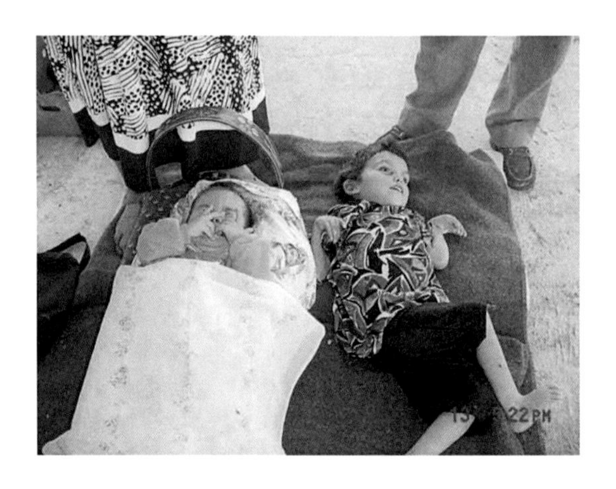

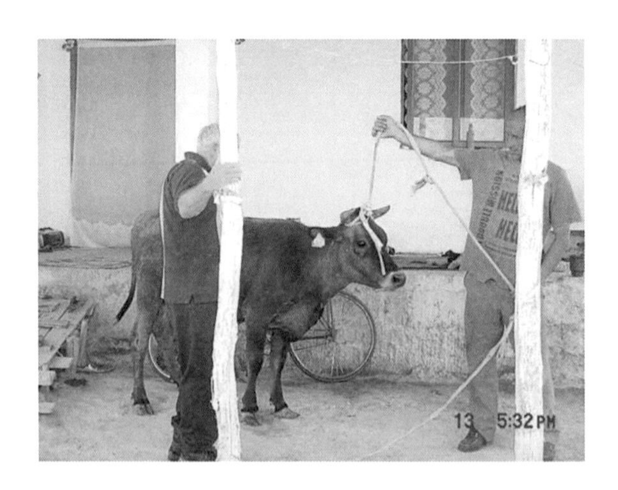

Friday, May 23, 2003

Greetings from Albania,

A month ago today we arrived in Albania. I tried to write yesterday. I had the letter almost finished when the electricity went off! (Talk about frustrating. We walked to the internet café. I had been typing about twenty minutes and lost it all.) So I will try again today.

We feel like we have made a good beginning in this first month. Three families have received cows. We have given close to 200 pair of socks away, plus medicine to different ones. Yesterday, Glen went looking for a car. He needs one to get to the villages. We still have have clothes, socks, medicine, Bibles and gospel literature to take to the villages or give to people we pass on the road. It won't take long to give what we brought away but we trust God to replenish the supply.

We are also making plans to take the "God's Story" video to different homes. Something else we started doing this week is to help Wendall (Canadian missionary) gather information about hotel rooms, advertising costs, renting the stadium here for a crusade this summer. That is another new experience for us.

We want to try and send you a letter each month to keep you informed. Thanks to everyone that has prayed for us and given to the mission.

God bless you!

****

Friday, May 30, 2003

Pam,

We are about to leave to go to two services in the village of Romanat. Glen bought a used car yesterday. He kept saying he wasn't going to pay over $2000. No one believed him but he finally found one. It is a 23 year old, white, Mercedes. He is going to have to get a set of tires because he already had a flat tire today. He said he thought those tires ought to last at least forty years like the shoes the Israelites wore in the wilderness! Ha!

Love you.........Sheila & Glen

****

Tuesday, June 24, 2003

Praise God for blessings by the bushel! Mark 4:24....And he said unto them, "Take heed what ye hear: with what measure ye mete, it shall be measured to you." How many blessings are you going to receive from the Word of God? When God measures them out to you He will be using your measuring stick. For instance, two people can hear the same message from the Word on healing. One will measure it with faith and one with skepticism. They will both receive what they believe. Jesus said, "Be it unto you according to YOUR faith!"

Can you believe it has already been two months since we arrived? Time is passing so rapidly! We feel that we have truly been blessed this month.

1) Glen bought a 23 year old Mercedes. So far, we have about $2,500 invested in it. When we leave, we plan on giving it to the young Albanian couple (Blerta and Ilir) that pastor and love to evangelize. Actually, we have already put it in his name. That way if we had to leave, everything would already be taken care of. In their own small towns they have shared the gospel in every home (as far as they know) and then branched out from there! Keep them in your prayers. Ilir is 27 years old and has never owned his own car. He rides his son to daycare on his bicycle. He helped Glen find the car. The day they bought it, it was very dirty. When Ilir got it to our house, he cleaned it inside and out just like we would treat a brand new car. Later that night, after we were in bed, we heard a knock at our gate. It was Ilir. He had brought some kind of sealant for the sunroof because he thought it might rain and he was afraid it might leak. They were both so excited. They can stand on their balcony and look down into our courtyard and see the car.

Blerta said she heard something the first night and she jumped out of the bed to go and check on the car. The next day we went to buy insurance. Ilir was behind the wheel. He had his head bowed and he said softly, "This is an answer to my prayers." We felt such a reverance and presence of God in the car. We will never forget that moment.

Glen, Ilir, Blerta and Joshua with new car!

2) Some of you have heard about Glen helping the family of the first milk cow, build a two room "house". We had

enough donations this month from Hilham Church of God and from Greenville Assembly of God to buy them a carpet and some vinyl. Koli, the invalid spends a lot of time on the floor or ground on a blanket, so we wanted something warm for him to lie on in the winter. You would love him. At first, I thought he didn't have a clue to what goes on. He's crippled and can't talk clearly. Only sounds that you can't understand. After getting to know him I realize he understands more than I thought. He loves for me to take pictures of him with the digital camera and to show them back to him. The day we went to measure the carpet, Dila said that since receiving the cow, good things have been happening to her. I asked her what color of carpet she wanted and the translator said she asked, "What color do you want?" I guess she wanted to please me. The rug we found is very pretty and covers the living area. We put vinyl with similar color in the cooking area. We thought we might have to buy them some hay for the winter but they already have a big haystack in their yard put up for the winter.

Bruna and Glen carry vinyl up to house.

3) Another neat thing happened. We met a missionary couple from Virginia, Willard and Melba, at a missionaries meeting. We had to leave early so we only got their first names. We didn't know where they lived or how to get in touch with them. We live in Durres and we met them in Tirana but we knew they lived in another city. We started feeling that the

next milk cow might go to someone in their area. We felt so strongly about it that we decided to go to the AEP (ministry for missionaries) office in Tirana and see if they could help us find this couple. When we walked in the office......there was Willard! I knew it was a God encounter. I got so excited in my spirit. While we were talking, (we hadn't said a word about the cow) Willard brought the subject up. It just so happened that a woman, that is a hard worker in his church, had her cow die that week. It is her main source of income. So pray that if she is the one that God will give us wisdom and direction.

4) You wouldn't believe the circles and hoops you have to jump through just to get a price on renting the stadium. The man who is supposed to be in charge said we needed to type a letter to the Mayor with specific dates and purpose. All this just to get an idea of what the cost is!

Well, the letter has finally been delivered and we are waiting for a reply.

5) Glen and I were walking down the street the other day and found "more than enough" money to pay our electric bill! He found 500 lek (approx. $5). We praise God in ALL things! Hallelujah!

The other night we heard a knock on our gate. Two little girls that we didn't know from Adam came to visit us. We treated them to some candy and a drink (Albanian custom) and talked to them the best we could. They were so cute sitting on the couch like little ladies. We gave them both a children's Bible, some socks, baby powder, and children's vitamins. Then the older one started teach me (Sheila) Albanian words. After she would teach me a few words she would test me! She's definitely teacher material. I think they would have stayed all night if Glen hadn't eased them on out. They came from a town several hours away to visit their family. Glen said God is sending them to US! We don't even have to step out the door! He makes things so easy for us.

7) A lady we met at Dila's home named Prena kept asking us to come visit her. She lives down the road from Dila. So we set up an appointment for yesterday at 5 pm to visit and show the God's Story video. Counting us, Glen said he counted around sixteen. Prena's husband doesn't go to church. Glen and I really took a liking to him. He was so nice to us. The house is small but very clean. Prena's mother-in-law lives with them. She looks very old but sometimes it is hard to tell here. They have six children. After about fifteen minutes the video started acting up. I had another one so we put it in but it acted up too! So we have to go back after we work out the problem. Glen and I believe someone else was supposed to be there. We will get to spend more time with them. We gave Prena a big Bible Story book plus everyone that needed a New Testament received one. We served them coke and cookies, but Prena still insisted on serving us their thick coffee. I managed to get mine down. Glen said he drank most of his. They were

proud of us. They like to toast every time you drink with them. They say, “Gezuar” which means “cheers”. We are gradually developing relationships.

8) Before we left the states a lady said she felt we would meet some important people. Saturday we are going to the U.S. Ambassador’s residence for a 4th of July party. All U.S. citizens are invited. I’ll write more on that next month. Glen said, “Who would have thought that two hillbillies would ever go to the ambassador’s residence?” Of course, we also are ambassadors for a greater country! Right?

9) We have stopped along roadsides and given out Bibles, socks, clothes…….whatever to people in hay wagons, auto repair shops, pedestrians, etc. It’s hard to remember everything. I (Sheila) found a piece of property that I would love to see a Praise and Worship center on. I call it my Prayer Mountain even though it is really just a hill. Hey! To a Florida girl it looks like a mountain!

We feel your prayers and are thankful for them and for each and every one of you. We are continuing to believe for bushel baskets of blessings. Are you?

****

Friday, July 4, 2003

Greetings to all of our fellow Americans! I am so glad to be born in America. Glen and I pray that you have a blessed day and pray for Revival in the Land of the FREE!

We went to the Fourth of July party at the American Ambassador's residence in Tirana. Everything was decorated so festive! The weather was perfect. Wish you had all been there. They had hamburgers, hotdogs, salads, chips, desserts (including apple pie) and all you could drink (non-alcoholic). It was so neat to be with so many fellow Americans that have a heart for Albania. The Ambassador gave a short five minute speech expressing his thanks to us for being in Albania at a time when Americans around the world are not always welcome. He was very gracious. He let us go in to his home to use the restrooms and look around. The most moving part of the day was when the Marine color guard marched out. It gave us chills! It was a perfect day. Thank you, Lord!

Glen standing by the podium where the ambassador spoke.

****

Friday, July 4, 2003

Hi girls, Ed & Herb,

I'm sending this to those that know us and will appreciate the humor.

Wednesday, Glen and I went back to the family that we had tried to show the God's Story video. We had made a picture of the man, wife, son and his 87 (?) year old mother. It was an 8X10 and we put it in a frame. The man was very touched (unbeliever). He is so nice. His name is Peter Prenga, also. I think he is related to Dila's husband, Peter. He went into his house and brought us both a cold, refreshing drink served in nice glasses on tray. He served it to us with a shy smile. His wife wasn't home. Normally, the woman does this. (It was really hot that day.) It looked like bubbling white grape juice to me. It turned out to be homemade beer from the grapes he grows! It was either that or wine or champagne. Not really sure. Not knowing what to do, we chugged it all down! Before we left they loaded us down with cucumbers, corn and peppers from their garden.

After we left there, we went to my hilltop. We worshipped God and had communion (grape juice). I could have used you girls. I poured the juice and threw some of the bread on the ground like Gwen Shaw teaches on redeeming the land. It was an awesome time. After we left there we went to Dila's house. They had seen us going up to my hill and Koli was shouting at us. It is usually them that we go out there to visit so we couldn't walk past them without stopping in. So, of course, we had to have another drink. This time we were served some orange drink. You need a large bladder to go visit Albanians unless you are going to make only one visit. They all insist on serving you a drink even if you aren't thirsty!

On our way home I was thinking about drinking that beer or whatever it was. I commented to Glen, "We would have really offended that man that we are trying to win if we had refused his drink." Glen said, "Yeah, but we really didn't have to drink that third jug!" I busted out laughing. I thought you guys would enjoy that one. Boy, do we have some experiences over here!

Sheila's hilltop

Saturday, July 26, 2003

Greetings from Albania,

Glen and I returned from Greece on Monday. We have to leave the country every three months because we don't have a residence permit. We went with another missionary couple from Canada, Wendall and Maureen and their two children. I guess you could say we were backpacking across Greece. At least, that is as close to backpacking as I care to do.

Getting ready to get on the bus to go from Kastoria to Thessaloniki. All of our clothing for the week is in our backpacks.

We have a good report from the Elbasan area. Since 1993 Glen has been sowing Bibles and aid into that area. Rick, Lisa and I went on one of those trips. I'm sure they will remember that bouncy ride. We were in a service a couple of weeks ago. An evangelist from Jacksonville, FL was preaching. Her name is Audrey Mack. She had been in a service the night before in Elbasan. She said there was an awesome move of God. People were saved, filled with the Spirit, slain in the Spirit, rejoicing in the Lord! Glen shared with the translator after the service how he had worked that area since 1993 and had wondered if any of his seeds had come up. The translator smiled and said, "For sure, your seed has come up." Glen was so encouraged. We praise God that every now and then He gives us a glimpse of the results of our labor.

Some of the churches in the states that contributed to these Bibles are: Highland Hills COG (school), New Vision COG, Greenville Assembly of God, Bolivar COG, Lake City COG, Grace Fellowship Assembly of God, and Northside COG, as well as individuals. We hope that these churches will be encouraged to know that their labor is not in vain.

God bless you all, Glen and Sheila

P.S. Something to pray about. Every night around 6:00 p.m. smoke starts blowing through our kitchen window. I told Glen maybe it is marijuana. We don't know what marijuana smells like but a neighbor said it smells like burning grass. Glen said he didn't think it was marijuana because if it was we would be "higher than a kite". I replied, "How do you know that we aren't and just don't know it? Maybe that is why we are so happy and the Christians three blocks away are always stressed and act miserable." We had a good laugh. Just pray that whatever it is, it will stop. If we start getting miserable after it stops I may have you pray for it to come back! (HA!)

****

Friday, August 8, 2003

Greetings from Albania,

We pray everything is going well with you in the states. Monday evening Blerta and Ilir went with us to Prena's house. God has put it on Glen's heart to buy Prena's girls and Dila's girls two outfits and shoes for school. When Blerta shared with Prena and Peter what Glen wanted to do, Prena said that she and her husband had been in anguish about what to do. Their girls didn't want to go to school because they are made fun of. They already have a strike against them because they are mountain people. There is a lot of prejudice in Albania. Prena shared how she wrapped plastic on her girls' shoes last winter (the rainy season) and they walked several miles every day to school and back. They didn't miss a day! The roads are unpaved and muddy when it rains where they live (and in a lot of Albania!). They live close to my favorite "hilltop". They have lived there for three or four years. They have a garden and a few goats. They lived in a tent the first year they were on the property and snakes would crawl in with them. (Yuck!) But she praised God for good health and six healthy children. She praised God for what Glen wants to do. (I pray that it is a witness to her husband that God cares and answers prayer.)

We also brought a suitcase full of socks, shoes and clothing. We told them to help themselves. Prena found a purple velvet dress that our friend Bobbie donated. She held it up to her and said, “Aah, in my old age I will be dressed like a bride!” She asked if she could call some of the neighbors’ children. We eagerly said, “Yes!” Prena loves children. She wasn’t going to just heap it all on herself. The mountain people are very polite and will refuse your help but Glen gives it to them anyway. These are the people he feels called to the most. (Maybe it is because he is a Tennessee mountain boy.)

Before we left, Prena insisted on going to her garden and loading us down with fresh tomatoes, peppers, corn, cucumbers and eggplant! Wow! Talk about an immediate harvest!

We will pick them up Thursday morning to go to the market. Thursday is Blerta and Ilir's day off. They will be a big help because they can barter and translate for us.

After we left there we still had a few items of clothing, socks and Bibles. We went to the well where many get their drinking water. It is one of Glen's favorite places to go. There were several teenage girls and boys there as well as children drawing water. Glen started giving out socks and soon the people were coming from every direction. It is still a mystery to me how they can find out we are there and get to us so quickly! We gave away every Bible, sock and piece of clothing. We gave out tracts, also. One man about forty years old asked Glen for a Bible. Glen had one left and was able to give it to him. We felt bad when we ran out of stuff to give, especially the children's Bibles. The people were still coming and asking for the books. We will have to go back! They asked if we were coming back. We like to go with Blerta and Ilir because they have a heart for evangelism and they are quite experienced to be so young. They definitely put me to shame in this area. I thank God for them. I pray God will raise up thousands just like them in Albania and around the world.

Keep us in your prayers. You are in ours. We love you.

God bless you......Glen & Sheila

Monday, August 11, 2003

Hello from Albania,
Thursday morning we took Prena and her girls to the market. They were all so happy (although the older girl is quiet and shy). We bought them two outfits, shoes, underclothing and each a book bag. I saw Prena try on a pair

of dress shoes and put them back. I couldn't resist getting them for her. Prena shared how she had prayed, "Lord, help my girls get what they need for school, especially Ela that is starting high school." After Peter heard what we were going to do he went to the school and registered his girls! I guess they wouldn't have gone to school this year if God hadn't moved on Glen's heart. Thank God for Glen's obedience. Keep this family in your prayers. We don't think Peter is a Christian (yet). We are going back to show the "God's Story" video when the weather cools. Pray that God will prepare hearts. We don't know if Peter's mother is saved, either.

When we got back to the car after our shopping, Ilir was stooped down witnessing to an older lady. Ilir prayed with her before leaving.

Well, after our shopping trip I asked Ilir to take me by the house to get my camera to take a picture of the girls and to check on Glen. He hadn't felt good all night (indigestion). Ilir had prayed for him before we left the house and God touched him. He was dressed and feeling fine when we got there. We had Prena and the girls come in and show Glen what they bought. They tried on their shoes for him. They were both already wearing a pair of their new pants. They wore them from the market. Even Prena had to try on her new shoes for Glen.

After Ilir and Glen took the girls home we took Blerta and Ilir to the bank to open up their first savings account. They didn't even know how. Glen has been teaching them that they need to try to save 5% of their pay. They both work six days (counting their duties on Sunday) and only make $300 per month between them. To save will be a real challenge. We opened the account with $100. They thought that you had to have a lot of money to put in the bank. Blerta was overcome with emotion when we got back to the car. She said no one had ever done so much for them. Her heart was full. They are tithers and givers. I told her it was part of their harvest from the seed they have sown. It was a good day. Praise the Lord!

Ilir, Joshua and Blerta in front of the bank.

Blerta immediately began sharing with her sister and friends about how important it was to save part of your money. They began saving even more than 5%!

The other day we were at a restaurant when a guy a block away machine gunned down a police commissioner and his driver while they were in the police vehicle. It is what they call a "blood feud" over here. God divinely protected us or we could have been there. We normally walk on the street where the shooting took place. We were with Wendall and Maureen and we decided to take a back street instead of the main street. We had just sat down when ambulances and police cars sped past us with sirens screaming! Keep us in your prayers. No telling how many times he has protected us and we didn't even know it. Thank God no bystanders were injured but the two men died.

God bless you all,
Sheila & Glen

****

Friday, August 29, 2003

It has been very hot here this month so one Tuesday morning Glen walked me to the market and I bought 15 fans, the pretty ones that fold out. I gave them to the ladies that showed up for the ladies meeting that afternoon. They were like kids! They inspected them, exchanged them, etc. but they were extremely pleased that I thought of them.

Last week there was a four night crusade here with an evangelist from Canada. The pastor in charge had many obstacles. His son almost died of a fever and both of his children were in the hospital! He also had an attack on his body. At the last minute the people in charge of the stadium cancelled our reservations! He had to make other arrangements. The list goes on. They seem to have one crisis after another. If this is a demonic attack then please pray for their protection and deliverance! In spite of the obstacles, there were healings of deaf ears, poor eyesight; a man paralyzed on one side was restored, a child's crooked feet straightened. So Praise God! Jesus is Lord!

Wednesday morning we drove to a town about an hour away called Lushnja. A pastor from Virginia "Willard" and his wife "Melba" have been helping us with the fourth milk cow. Wednesday was the big day! This cow has a little bull calf so that is a bonus. The woman who received this cow is "Jasmina". She is a dedicated Christian and a hard worker for the church. She has two daughters and a son. Her husband is an unbeliever and addicted to alcohol. She had twenty turkey eggs that didn't hatch. She planted corn for her cow and the corn died. Then her cow, which is her main source of income, died! She said that she felt like giving up but determined to trust God. The week her cow died is the week God divinely appointed us to meet Willard and Melba. Glen shared with them what he was doing with milk cows. Then later that week, Willard found out about Jasmina's cow dying. Willard remembered Glen and his "cow" ministry. He didn't know where we were living. God ordered our steps and his to the same office, on the same day that we were looking for him and he was looking for us! Praise the Lord! Even though he lives in Lushnja and we live in Durres, we met each other in Tirana, so I believe the whole thing was ordained by God. Pray that this gift will soften Jasmina's husband's heart and he will accept Jesus. That is the most important thing.

We named the cow and calf, "Big Barb" and "Little Herbie" after our friends that donated it.

Jasmina with "Big Barb" and "Little Herbie"

This morning, as I write this letter, Glen is out visiting new people and giving out more socks, clothes and Bibles. When he returns we will walk to an internet café and hopefully, send this letter. One thing for sure, I've learned to hit save often just in case the power shuts down! Guess I'm like Jesus. Jesus Saves!

****

Tuesday, September 2, 2003

Well, we had a busy morning. We went to visit a couple of new families as well as Dila and Prena.

It was quite a hike up to the first place. Praise God, I made it! This is a Muslim family that we hope to develop a relationship with and show the God's Story sometime in the near future. They had a houseful. There were four adults and seven children! We took the shoe sizes of the ones that are going to start school but we may buy a few extra pair for the little ones. This place had a "moonshine" still or what they call "raki" pronounced "rocky". No wonder Glen feels so at home here. They make raki on top of their Rocky Top! They offered us some but you will be glad to hear that we abstained.

Raki Still

The other new place we went to is up on the first hill that I climbed back in April. It wasn't as difficult this time. Maybe God is giving me my hind's feet! Long before we got to where we parked the car some children recognized Glen's car and started running after us and calling out to their friends. By the time we parked we had a good crowd! I know how Jesus felt when He crossed in a boat to the other side and by the time he got there the crowd was waiting on Him! Of course, the kids are interested in the goodies.....sound familiar? Isn't that why the crowd came after Jesus for much of the time? But, he didn't care. He had an audience and that was why he came.......to seek and to save that which was lost.

****

Tuesday, September 30, 2003

Hello friends and family,

September started off with a bang! God gave Blerta two weeks off so we hired her as a translator. She was upset at first about not working for two weeks but it was definitely a blessing in disguise for all of us. We did a lot of visitation in Tirana and Durres. We saw old friends and met some new ones. We bought school clothing, book bags, eyeglasses, shoes, Bibles, as well as food for needy families with donations from the states. We helped Blerta to get set up to teach English classes in her home to earn extra income. Glen kept preaching to Blerta and Ilir to save some of their income. They caught hold of it they said because Glen kept pushing them. Then they preached it to Blerta's sister that lives several hours away. She caught on and went home and began preaching it to her friends. Something so elementary to us is an exciting new concept to them.

September 8th was the BIG day scheduled to go back to Prena's and try to show the God's Story again. The morning was beautiful just like almost every day has been since we arrived. We were scheduled to go with Blerta, Ilir and little Joshua to Prena's at 5:30 p.m. We lay down to rest around 2:00 p.m. (a custom over here that I really like) and when we got up it was lightly raining. (Brother Johnson came that week. He said it was his fault. It rains wherever he goes.) Prena's road is hard to drive on in dry weather, but a little rain makes it close to impossible. Ask Brother Johnson, we took him on it as far as we could and had to turn around before we got to our destination. I wanted to cancel but my persistent husband pulled me through. We loaded up with our video, DVD player, snacks, (no umbrella), and some "doubts" (not Glen). It started raining harder!! Blerta and I kept shooting glances at each other. We got to this one curve and Glen had to get out and push because the car was sliding toward a steep bank. We still had the worst curve and steepest bank ahead of us and the old enemy named "Fear" whispered, "It is going to be dark by the time you leave Prena's." On the final curve, Blerta, Joshua and I got out of the car. Glen was already out pushing the car. There was a steep bank on the right that ends in a water reservoir. Glen wanted us to stay in the car but "Fear" said, "That's easy for him to say. He's not in the car. You are the one that is going to slide into the reservoir, not him!" So we trudged the last couple of blocks in the rain and mud. Some children from Prena's came running up the road with umbrellas, all excited about the video. Two of the children were from a Muslim home. When we got in to the small living room there were about fifteen of us all together. The owner's elderly mother was there, which is one of the reasons that Glen was so persistent. He was concerned about her leaving this world without an opportunity to hear the gospel. When we started showing the video (on a tiny, little portable DVD player) it started raining so hard that Prena had to close the window so that we could hear the video. Prena said we needed to stay the night there because the road would be too bad. I finally got a grip. I began confessing under my breath, "Thank you Lord that we will all sleep safe and sound in our **own** beds tonight. I am blessed going out and I am blessed coming **IN**."

Everyone watched the video attentively. Glen served snacks and drinks while the video was playing to save time. Afterwards, Ilir spoke to them for about five minutes exhorting them that Jesus is the only way. They all said that they believe and prayed the sinner's prayer. The seed has been sown. Glen and I are continuing to visit and encourage them. The rain had let up to a light drizzle. Blerta and I stayed in the car on the way back down the hill. Prena's husband, son and daughter pushed us for about ten minutes. We all slept safe and sound in our own beds that night. We had a sweet peace because this family had heard the gospel. Also, when we arrived at Prena's our shoes were caked in mud. When I got home I noticed my shoes were clean. Unknowing to us they had cleaned our shoes when we were in the house. You always take your shoes off before entering the house.

Group gathered to watch the God's Story video.

The next week we spent in Macedonia. We were blessed by the Church of God to go to a minister's conference for all the Balkan nations. We only had to provide transportation. They paid for everything else. It was an anonymous gift given for a minister's conference. God even took care of the transportation. We had been praying on how to get there when we were contacted by a couple from Mississippi that has been missionaries to Hungary for twelve years. They were so gracious to offer us to ride with them. Their names are Dan and Rose. They have two beautiful children. God called them to Albania for one year to pray and intercede for Albania! What a blessing they have been to us.

Glen ended the month on a high note. While I was taking my Albanian class, Glen and Ilir went visiting in three homes that he wants to show the video. He had made plans with Ilir to leave after Ilir got off work. About an hour before time to leave it started to drizzle rain but Glen proceeded to load up the car anyway. (We could all learn from my husband.) When it was time to leave the rain had stopped. Glen bought fresh loaves of bread to give to the families as well as some Bibles and clothing. The highlight for him was when he gave a little fella a brand new pair of sneakers. He said the little guy strutted all over the house, proud as a peacock. Wow! What a wonderful, blessed month we had!! Praise God!

****

Tuesday, October 7, 2003

Well today is kind of a sad day for us. Our backpacking buddies from Canada.... Wendall, Maureen, Katon and Kesa are on their way to the Tirana airport. They have been here one year and are on their way home. We wish them all the best. They will be sorely missed!

Friday, October 31, 2003

Greetings to family and friends. Our thoughts and prayers are with you. We are so blessed that you are in our life. It has rained almost every day this month but today, October 31, the sun is shining brightly. As I write this draft letter, Glen is sitting on the porch trying to soak up some much needed sunshine.

We started out the month by saying goodbye to our Canadian backpacking buddies. What a neat family! We hated to see them go. Their apartment is next door to us and it seems so silent now. We used to hear their children playing with the missionary children from Holland. It seemed to affect the little boy from Holland the most. His mother saw him looking out the window one day, staring at the empty apartment. He turned to his mother and said, "I miss them so much!" Children on the mission field are also giving up their life for the gospel. We need to remember them in our prayers and thank them. Then, yesterday we said goodbye to a couple we have come to love and appreciate, Willard and Melba from Virginia.

Willard recently turned 70 years young and he has more energy and can work circles around men half his age. Melba goes places that I wouldn't even attempt! They both seem to glow with health as well as with the Spirit. What an encouragement they have been to us. They are planning on returning next May.

Willard and Melba

The middle of October we went to a missionary conference in Macedonia. Dan Smith and his son Daniel graciously allowed us to ride with them. Missionaries from all over Albania and Kosovo attended. It was fun to hear how God was using different missionaries. The best story I heard was from a lady in Kosovo. She told us about a little girl about five years old that had to have heart surgery. A church in Greenville, SC sponsored her. She flew to America with her mother and translator. The doctor didn't give much hope. He hesitated about doing the surgery. He wasn't a believer but the church told him that they were going to pray that God would give him the wisdom to perform the surgery. The little girl had seen the Jesus film. The night before the surgery she asked to watch it again. She and her mother accepted Christ. When the father called that night the mother told him what she had done. He prayed to God, "God if you heal my little girl, I will believe in you and serve you." As the child was wheeled into surgery she was not afraid. She said that she knew she was going to be okay because God told her He had a work for her to do. Praise God the surgery was a success! After the child returned to Kosovo the missionary went to see her. The house was full of relatives. The relatives wanted to know why the child, her parents and siblings were so joyful and full of peace. The missionary shared the gospel.

When she was finished someone asked her, "Do you have to go to America to receive this peace?" She said, "No, anyone can receive it, right now." All the relatives accepted Christ! (I think she said about 18 but I am not sure of the exact number, a large group.) They now have church in this town. This is a Muslim community! Praise God!

We haven't been able to get to the homes in the village to show the "God's Story" video this month because the rain makes it impossible for me to get up to their homes. Of course, my mountaineer husband has trudged up there alone and brought the families bread and talked with them. He has also checked on the cows and on some goats. We showed the video in our home on Tuesday night to a couple of young women. They live across the street. Their family is Muslim. They were really touched but said they want to think about it before they make such a serious commitment. (Blerta translated for us.) Keep them in your prayers. The seed has been sown and I know it won't return void. Their names are Erjola and

Zamira. We gave them both a Bible and a gospel tract.

We have started working on our Christmas gift bags. We are going to take some to the villagers and some to a small COG congregation in Marikaj. There are a lot of handicapped people in this church. Also, pray that God will bless them with an overhead projector as well as their own building.

Here are some interesting facts I read in the book, "The Last of the Giants". I quote:.......foreign missions remain a poor sideshow when it comes to Christian spending habits. Whereas the average Christian family income in 1990 was $19,280, the weekly foreign missions giving per church member was a paltry ten cents. Moreover, most of what is given in the name of "missions" today, at least in America, is used to propagate the Gospel among people who have the opportunity to hear the Good News up to one hundred times each day. Only 0.1 percent of all Christian income is spent on direct ministry outside the

Christianized world------and a microscopic 0.01 percent on the hardcore unevangelized world."

I have to admit that I cringe inside when I read such statistics. It is time that we re-evaluate not only our personal spending but as a Church body we may need to come up with a new distribution plan of our church income. Think about it and if you are really brave...PRAY about it! If you could see a pie chart of your church's last year's income and how it was divided up you might be shocked!

I know many of you are planning on going on different missions trips. Here is a tip. Pack light for yourself but be sure to use all your allowed baggage. You are usually allowed two large checked bags plus your carryon luggage. Fill them with goodies to give away. Glen and I paid $70.00 per extra suitcase above our allowed baggage. So if you are allowed two suitcases, plus your carry on and you only bring one suitcase for yourself then that is like throwing away $70.00. If ten people did that, that would be $700.00! If you know of missionaries that you will see, contact them to see if there is anything special they might need. Our son and daughter-in-law just sent us a small package. It was expensive. If they had known someone that was coming this way they could have filled a large suitcase for just a little more than what they paid for a small box (even though it seemed like a large box to us it was small in comparison to a large suitcase). This is just a tip for all of you future travelers. Even though it is a hassle to keep up with your luggage, I think it is good stewardship to take advantage of the entire luggage you are allowed to bring.

In His service................Sheila and Glen

P.S. A bunch of celery costs $5.85! During the day we have approximately five hours of electricity, off and on. Sometimes it takes two or three hours to do one load of wash!

Sunday, November 30, 2003

The month of November flew by! We have been preparing the gift bags to give out for

Christmas. Glen has made several trips to the village and brought the people bread and just spent time with them. We also save our empty one liter water bottles and when we get a large trash bag full, Glen takes them to Dila to put her milk in to sell. Her cow is giving plenty of milk. Praise the Lord! There is still one family up there that we want to show the video to. Pray that we will be sensitive to the Holy Spirit and go in His perfect timing. We ended the month with a trip to Corfu, Greece. It is a beautiful island across from Albania. We went with the couple from Vermont that needed to get away for a much needed rest. They will be responsible for Durres Christian Center while David and Valbona are in Canada. Keep them in your prayers.

Have a joyful Christmas and a prosperous New Year. We love you and miss you.
Sheila and Glen

Tuesday, December 30, 2003

Glen and I want to wish you a blessed and prosperous 2004! We can't believe how quickly 2003 has passed.

The month of December started out beautiful! Clear and cool but not too cold. This was an answer to prayer because on December 4th Glen had an appointment to go up into a mountain village with Vita and Ermir. They could only drive so far and then had to walk because the vehicle wouldn't make it with all of them because the ruts in the road were too deep and the vehicle would bottom out. They were bringing boxes from Samaritan's purse. They first gave them out at a school, then they sang and the pastor preached. Then they trekked off to three other homes to give boxes and have a service in the homes. Two other young men had come with them to help. It was early morning when Glen left and after dark when he returned. He was tired but very happy! He said it was the best day he has had this year! Wow! Vita told Glen that Ermir loves this village so much. He has been visiting and praying for a church in this village for three years! Glen hopes to help him realize his vision. Two weeks later, Glen, the pastor and some boys trekked back up there. This time Glen rented three donkeys. They loaded two with Bibles, shoes and clothing that we were able to donate thanks to many of you. The third donkey they took turns riding. They had a little Bible study with some children at the school and then went back to some homes and gave out coats, shoes and clothing. We knew for two weeks that Glen was going back so we began to pray and ask God to give us clear weather all week so that the path wouldn't be slippery and also we wanted clear weather for that Sunday because we had gift bags prepared to give out at the church. Praise God, He is faithful to hear our cry. The weather was clear Tuesday-Sunday! Monday we awoke to the sound of rain.

Arrive in village two and half hours later.

Glen was concerned he wouldn't have enough gift bags prepared but we had enough for the church and then after church, Glen and Ilir went to some of the homes we have been visiting and gave bags to the children. He still had three bags left. Ilir asked him did he want to take them back into the house. Glen said no that he would give them to someone the next day. The next day he was praying that God would show him who to give them to. He saw two adults and a little boy digging in the garbage. He stopped and gave each of them a bag. He also gave a little toy truck that he had left to the little boy. The little boy ran home with a BIG smile on his face. The beggars that we see with their children out in the weather are the ones that really tear at my heart. Pray that God will keep these little ones safe, warm and well. So, Glen said, "Once again God has provided more than enough"!

We spent Christmas Eve at the home of missionaries "Raymond and Wilna" with "Child Evangelism Fellowship". Their facility is about a half block from where we live. (God put us in such a great location. We are surrounded by missionaries!) We shared fellowship, food, songs and prayer. There were missionaries from Korea, Austria, Ireland, Holland, Sweden, England and Tennessee (that is part of the USA for those of you who may be wondering....ha!). They asked the different missionaries to sing a carol in their "native" tongues. It was beautiful to hear the different languages, especially the children. The only song that I could think of in the "Tennessee" language was "Rocky Top"! This is kind of appropriate for Albania. It has lots of rocks and they call their moonshine "rocky" (raki)! No, we didn't sing it but I think they probably would have had a good laugh if we had. *Raymond (the host) said next year they all expect to hear a song in "our" language. Hmmm.....what do you think? Do we dare? Let me know. I need some really "spiritual" input on this one! ***(Home with Jesus on March 16, 2010).**

Today is December 29th. It is clear and warmer, which is good because the electricity has been off more than on the past couple of weeks. Albanians are gearing up for their biggest celebration which is New Years. That is when they cook their turkeys (which are really expensive) and have family get-togethers. Blerta and Ilir want us to spend New Year's Eve with them. The custom is to spend it with the husband's parents. Since Ilir's father left when he was small he doesn't have a father to spend it with. We will fill in for him. We really love this Godly young couple.

January 13, 2004

Good morning everyone! It is a beautiful day in Albania! I have a story to share with you. In the summer of 2002 I read an article in Perry Stone's magazine called "Give For the Crown" (or something like that). I felt depressed after reading it (This is no reflection on Perry. I love his ministry.) In the article it talked about how we would be embarrassed when we got to heaven if we didn't have a crown to give to Jesus. The part about being embarrassed is what depressed me. A day or so later my husband and I were in bed and I read the article to him. Then I shared my fear of not having a crown and being embarrassed. I told him that I had said to the Lord, "Lord, I have had enough embarrassment down here. I didn't know I might be embarrassed up there! I already suffered the embarrassment of having an alcoholic father (whom I loved dearly), having to wear glasses since I was a child (back in those days not many wore glasses) and having the kids call me 4-eyes, having kids call me names because of an overbite (I still cringe when I hear the words buck teeth or beaver), poor complexion.....I mean the list goes on and on! Now, I might be embarrassed in Heaven if I don't have a crown! I give up!" As I was sharing this with my husband (he is lighthearted and humorous whereas, I tend to be more serious) he patted me on the arm and said, “That’s okay honey, if you don’t have a crown then I will give you one of mine”. I busted out laughing. We have had many laughs over this since then.

A few weeks later, my friend Bobbie was at my home and she was going through a very difficult time. I shared with her how I had felt when I read this article and she admitted that she had felt the same way when she read it. Then I shared with her what Glen had said and she roared with laughter which she really needed. Then one night Glen and I were watching the news and we saw the pope. He had on his hat that he wears and his head was leaning to the side. Glen said, “Look at him Sheila. His crown is so heavy it makes his head tilt to the side.” Then one Sunday afternoon we were at a church dinner at Parkwest COG and we were enjoying fellowship with Joe Christian. We started talking about Brother T.L. Lowery and how much we admired him. (Joe didn’t know anything about my crown story.) He made the remark, “Yep, they are going to have to have a semi-truck to hold Brother Lowery’s crowns.”

Glen and I agreed and just looked at each other. It was all I could do not to burst out laughing.

When our pastors Rick and Lisa were with us in Albania last year we were eating at a restaurant and I began telling them about my concerns over not having a crown. I shared all of the above with them and we had a good laugh. Since then, Rick has made reference to a crown from the pulpit and would look at me. Now you at CMC know why. I have even emailed him asking him did he think the things I have been doing in Albania were adding to my crown.

So, we have had a good time (at my expense I might add) with this story. Well, this morning Glen took a picture of my "BEST" Albanian crown. When he saw me he remarked, "I like your crown". I am attaching the picture for you. Herb will you make a copy of this letter and give it to Joe Christian? Tell him the two suitcases beside me are full of my other "lesser" crowns! Not a semi-truck yet, but it is a donkey load! Praise God! Hallelujah! I won't have to hang my head down when I get to Heaven! Glory to

God! Those who trust in HIM will NEVER be ashamed!

I just wanted to share this little story with you all. I hope it will bring a smile to your face and maybe even a little chuckle.

P.S. This is no reflection on Perry's article. The point he was making is that we need to give with the right attitude and motives.

Sheila's Crown

Sunday, January 25, 2004

Greetings from Albania! It sure is cold outside! Brrrrrr!!!

January literally started off with a BANG!!! New Year's Eve is their biggest holiday. Albanians fly home from Italy for this time of year. We were told the first ten days of January it is their custom to make visits to all the family members. We watched the fireworks from our bedroom window. Everyone was shooting them. It looked like they were shooting each other and sounded like a war! On January 4th Glen opened up a savings account for Vita and Ermir. Just like Blerta and Ilir they had no idea how to do this. They were so appreciative and blessed.

Back in October we received an email about a few people that were concerned over the abortion situation in Albania. They wanted to hear from anyone else who was concerned. I planned on emailing them but never did. A couple of months later, one night I couldn't sleep. I started looking at different things that were in my Bible cover. I came across a poster and some brochures from years ago on abortion. As I looked at the little aborted babies I began to weep. A day or so later, I picked up an old notebook that I brought with me from the states. I started to tear out a sheet that had some writing on it and throw it away. Then I thought, "I should see what it says." It was a Word from the Lord that I had received on abortion in September of 1992! I thought, "Lord, are you trying to get my attention?" A few nights later Blerta and Ilir were over. I asked them had they ever seen an aborted baby. They said, "No". So I showed them the poster I had. They were shocked! So I emailed the people in Tirana and said I would like to meet with them. On January 14th, Glen and I met with them in a restaurant. It is always a challenge to ride into Tirana and I almost backed out. I'm so glad I didn't. Abortion is a real problem here. Some women have had over twenty abortions! I believe it was the "beginning" of a pro-life movement here. I don't know why, but God lets me in on the beginning of things, many times. Despise not the day of small beginnings! It was encouraging to all of us. We had a time of prayer and shared different ideas.

Our first pro-life meeting.

I had a ladies' Bible Study at my house the next day and needed some snacks. When we went to check our mail at the AEP office, we had an unexpected package from Glen's brother, Raymond that was filled with snacks! Even my favorite, "Chex Mix" was in it. While we were waiting for the two ladies to arrive for our abortion meeting I made the comment to Glen that I wish we would see Larry and Janice while we were in Tirana. When our meeting was wrapping up, in walked Larry and Janice! God is so good to me! (Glen thinks he's God's pet but I am beginning to wonder. Hmmm....could it be someone with the initials SDW?)

The next day we woke up to dark, angry looking clouds and strong winds. Glen was supposed to go to the mountain village with Ermir. It is a two and a half hour walk. He considered not going but he pushed himself. I thought for sure he would return in an hour it looked so bad outside. It looked that way all day but none of the group (Glen, Ermir, Vita and infant) ever got wet! The pastor testified Sunday that when he saw Glen drive up that morning it gave him the courage to obey God and go in faith. He said to himself, "If that "old man" can do it so can I because I am a young man." A teenager testified that he fasted and prayed for them that day while he was at school, asking God to keep them safe and dry. When the small group of four plus two donkeys arrived in the village they saw a young boy about 13 years old waiting for them. Vita said, "Do you know that we are having a meeting at the school today?"

He said, "Yes, that is why I am here waiting on you. You promised to bring back a Bible to me on January 15th." When the young mother heard this, joy filled her heart and she said the hard trip had been worth it. When they arrived at the school the "director" said they weren't supposed to have a religious meeting there but to go ahead and use a certain room that he took them to. They had a wonderful time of preaching and singing.

On the 16th, Glen and I were walking to the bank to deposit some money in Vita and Ermir's account. I had their account number but I thought to myself, "It would be nice to have his account book so that it would be entered in his book. They don't live in our city but as we were walking we saw this couple! They had just been to the bank and so they had their savings book with them! Once again God gave me my desire. If we had left five minutes sooner or later we would have missed them. God's timing was perfect.

God supplied more funds so Glen bought a milk goat for a family on the 16th. Ilir went with him to translate. While they were in that area they visited the family that received the first cow. The owner said the cow was sick. Glen and Ilir went and prayed for the cow. A day or so later a neighbor of theirs made a special trip to town to let Glen know that the cow is doing fine! Thank you, Lord!

Friday was the coldest day we have had thus far. We went to the mountain city of Kruja to visit some friends. Dan and Rose Smith and their children, Daniel and Marion Grace have been sent to this city for a year to intercede for Albania. They have been given a difficult assignment but God has prepared them and knows that He can trust them. Whenever they come to your mind lift them up to the Lord. Dan will be in Hungary for the last two weeks of February. Rose will be holding down the fort. Please remember them. We have been blessed to know this couple. They are from Mississippi and have been missionaries to Hungary for many years, but Dan's "first love" is Albania.

Yesterday we went to visit Blerta's parents. When we arrived it was about 32 degrees in the apartment! The power was off. They have a small gas heater but they didn't have any gas in it. In a short while they had bought or borrowed a tank from somewhere. Blerta's mother insisted on serving us a meal. She prepared a whole meal on a portable gas "one" burner "thing a ma jig", two meats, boiled eggs, salad, bread, cheese and olives. She wanted to fry us potatoes but we said it was too much already. Then she served cake! We were stuffed. She said if she had known we were coming she would have fixed a big meal! Thank God we surprised her!!!

In Albania, people are always starting a new business. If one person is doing good selling produce then six more people on the same block will open a little stand. So Glen and I have decided to start a new business. Since life in Albania is so "easy" and "worry free", uh-huh. We are going to open a "worry" business for our fellow Americans that have such a "hard" life! Instead of you worrying, for $5.00 an hour we will do your worrying for you. We may have to charge a little extra for those "big worries", like which restaurant should we go to or where will we go on vacation this year? Jarvis, since you are more experienced in this department Glen wants you to come over to be our "project manager"! We have named our business, "Glen and Sheila's Don't Worry Be Happy Inc.". Just sent your worries to us!

Glen and Sheila's new business. FYI the jugs are the maple syrup jugs we received when we first arrived.

****

We ended up having to leave for the states a couple of months ahead of schedule. The people that were renting our home left without notice in the middle of winter! We were concerned the pipes would bust. It was hard to leave Blerta and Ilir but it was the right decision. We gave them our Tennessee sweatshirts before we left. It would be over a year before we would see them again.

Blerta and Ilir our “Vols” in Albania.

Chapter 7

He Hath Done Great Things!

Since the last chapter God has done so many wonderful things. I don't have enough room to tell it all. I told Sheila we will have to write another book! Nevertheless, there are a few things I just have to share. I will write in more detail in the next book.

As of this writing, January 25, 2010 we have given away thirty-three milk cows and they each have a story. I will try to squeeze the "2005" cows in to this book.

****

May 19, 2005

Hello to our friends and family in America! Great is the Lord and greatly to be praised. We trust that you have had a blessed week. Blessed going out and blessed coming in! We interviewed some families last week and we praise God that on Wednesday we blessed two families with a cow.

The first family is a widow and three children. She is in her early thirties and her name is Dhuretta. Her husband had been working in Italy, trying to get ahead, when last August he was killed in an auto accident. He was only 32 years old. Since he wasn't working in Albania the widow has no pension. She has been making bread to earn a little income. She has about $40 a month coming in. She is a dedicated Christian and had been praying for about a year that God would give her a cow! The cow we gave her is pregnant. The name of the cow is Shay Shay. We prayed with her after she received the cow and she was praising God and so happy!

Before Glen gave away the next cow the Holy Spirit asked him, "What will you do when the person you buy a cow from is in greater need than who you plan on giving it to?" So, he had been thinking about it.

The next cow we gave is "Krista". It was given to a family of eight. Glen was interviewing this man about buying his cow. The man didn't really want to sell his cow but he explained to Glen that he had to sell it to pay his grocery bill. Glen's heart was so touched. Then the man asked him, "What needy family are you going to give the cow to?" Glen turned his head away for a moment as tears came to his eyes. He turned back and said, "We are going to give the cow to you!" Praise God! They had one little boy that has a crippled foot. He stuck right with Glen. We had quite a hike to get to this cow. We drove as far as we could, then we walked for another twenty or thirty minutes. It was up there with the mountain goats. When Glen first pointed out where we were going, I confess I had some doubts. Praise God, I made it with no problem. God is good! All the time! When we got up to the cow we could look out over the Adriatic Sea! It was a beautiful sight to behold. On our way home we had a flat tire. We thank God that it was on a village road and that Ilir was with us, instead of on the highway by ourselves. Thank you, Jesus!

"Krista"

Glen is with Ilir right now, checking on some more cows. It is 6:23 pm. They had to go check on getting another tire before they go and check on the cows. We like to wait until Ilir gets home from work before we go because he speaks a little English and knows his way around.

When we went to our bank today to withdraw some money for cows, the lady that waited on us told us that she had told Ilir that she likes us. She said that Glen and I transmit or emanate tranquility, a peace! This blessed me very much. I praise God that the people recognize something different about us even if they don't understand what it is. Pray that the people will always sense His presence and see Him and not us.

May 27, 2005

Bless the Lord, Oh my soul and ALL that is within me BLESS His Holy Name! Great is the Lord and greatly to be praised for He has done great things!

Does it sound like we are rejoicing? For sure we are! Wednesday evening between the hours of 5:30 and 8:30 we bought and gave out the last three cows. That makes nine cows that have been given to the Albanian people through

Arise Shine Albanian Ministry! It would not have been possible without YOU! Thanks be to God for all of you.

We know that you have been praying for us. Wednesday morning, we knew we needed to find and buy two more cows. We weren't sure who we were going to give the last two cows to. We had three families and only two cows. Glen prayed that God would let him know for sure that he had made the right decision. At the end of the evening we passed by the family's house that we had not bought a cow for. We saw a cow in their yard! So they evidently had a cow already. It gave us peace to know we had given it to a family that had no cow.

The first cow we gave was cow number seven, "Grace"! The family that received this cow has three children and they live next to or maybe "in" the garbage dump. The mother and father both have physical disabilities. "Grace" has a calf and so the previous owner is going to keep her for three more weeks. This will give the calf more time to grow and be with her mother. It will also give the new owner more time to prepare a place for "Grace"! We hope to show God's Story to this family and to encourage them in the Lord.

They collect glass bottles from the dump and sell them for a living.

Family that received "Grace".

The eighth cow is "Destiny". God gave Barb and me a Word for this family before we came to Albania. This family is 'destined' for a "New Beginning"! They live across from Dila (The family that received the first cow.) Dila had been giving them a bottle of milk every morning. When we bought the fifth cow, the wife of this family had been there and requested a cow. At the time we thought we were going to give it to another family. She told us Wednesday when we gave her "Destiny" that she had told her three children to pray, pray, pray! Her face was shining when she received the cow. Her husband suffers from diabetes. Her name is Tone' and his is Pashk.

Lady in blue dress received "Destiny" the 8th cow.

The ninth cow is "Daisy"! When we visited the lady that received this cow (Marta), my heart went out to her. Her husband is unsaved and an alcoholic. Many times she comes to church bruised from his abuse. She broke down and cried when the man with us asked about her husband. Her church has been praying for his salvation. We didn't think we were going to give the cow to her when we visited that day. We told her we would be in prayer. She looked so depressed and hopeless when we left. Tuesday, we still didn't plan on giving her the cow. Then Wednesday afternoon when Blerta got off work she told us Marta knew where a cow was and wanted to give a little toward the cow if she received it! She was like the woman with the issue of blood that would not be denied! We were so impressed with her determination and her industrious attitude to go out and find a cow that we felt it was God answering our prayers and yours to be led by Him. Not only that, but Daisy is expecting! She should have the calf next month (I think). Hallelujah! I am so glad that Marta received "Daisy". She has gone through so much, just like the woman that donated the cow. After we paid for "Daisy", Marta was going to walk her home. We had to go take some pictures of the other cows and it was getting dark. We told Marta we would meet her at her house and take a family picture for her after we took the other pictures if it wasn't too late. It was almost dark when we finished and we almost decided to go on home, but I said she might be waiting for us so we needed to swing by and take her picture. Thank God we did! She was waiting outside the gate and she was upset! Although, we had the lady that we bought the cow from to count the money twice, Glen noticed he had a $100 and he didn't know where it was from. He said, "I hope we counted the money out right." Well, it turned out that we hadn't and Marta had walked home without "Daisy". Her children said, "Mama, come in the house." She said, "No, I am going to wait out here until they come." She was so distressed. We told her to get back in the car and we drove back to the owners of "Daisy" and apologized. They were afraid that we would think they were trying to pull something on us. We were concerned that they would think we had deliberately shorted them. Praise God everything worked out fine. Marta's face was shining and she was so happy to walk her cow home even though it was almost dark by then. Her countenance had "hope" now instead of despair. I told her we had been praying for her husband and believe for his salvation. She was so grateful. The enemy tried one more time to make her lose her "peace" but he is the "loser"! Praise God! We were praising God that we had made the effort to go back and check on Marta. If we had given in to our flesh, no telling how long she would have waited outside the gate for us. God definitely was in control of our steps on Wednesday afternoon and evening!

Marta in red pants receives "Daisy".

There is so much more that happened on this trip but I don't have room. We did buy one more cow that Sheila and I donated from our family. It would be the tenth cow and we donated it on June 10th. We named her "Sierra Joy" which means song of joy. We named her calf "Junebug". Sheila's niece Paula "Joy" and her sister Sheryl donated "Junebug". Of course, the names "Junebug" and "Sierra" are in memory of our "Junebug" and baby "Sierra".
They were given to a widow named "Tereza" that has three children. She lives with her in-laws.

******

In 2006 we helped Blerta and Ilir start a church "New Beginnings Fellowship". Our daughter-in-law "Pam" and our grandson "Chris" plus our cousin "Jeff" were in the very first meeting which was in Blerta's & Ilir's apartment. Jeff preached the meeting. Also, Vita and Ermir were there and Joshua.

Pam & Chris on far left. Jeff in white pants and dark shirt.

Many of the people that came in the beginning were people that we had been visiting since 2003. We brought our pastors "David and Almeda" over in 2007 to celebrate our first anniversary. It was an awesome time. The church was alive and growing. We had a baptism service where over twenty people were baptized.

First anniversary service.

Baptism

We've had our highs and lows since then but we continue to press on. In 2008 God put another village on our heart named "Prenjas". It is about three hours from Durres. That is where we spent much of our time in 2009. We feel the time is short and still so many that are unreached! We hear in our spirits, **John 9:4 "I must work the works of him that sent me, while it is day: the night cometh, when no man can work."**

And so.....while it is "day" the work will continue.

Seeds of Love

Seeds of Love is the story of a man that grew up in the hills of Tennessee, the son of a share cropper. With limited education but faith in a great God he is able to retire early and devote his life to the people in the once isolated nation of Albania. Read how God prepares him for his "destiny". Walk with him as he shares his journey filled with joyful experiences as well as great sorrow. Always pressing on to what God has called him to do. Sowing seeds of love to the poorest nation in Europe.

Sheila and Glen Watson
Arise Shine Albanian Ministry

Sheila and Glen have attended Pentecostal churches for the past thirty-eight years. They have five children, thirteen grandchildren and three great-grandchildren. They live in Loudon, Tennessee. They aren't ordained ministers. They are two people that have a heart for world missions and especially for Albania.

This is the Sunday School Group.

This is the 40th milk cow bought in Albania. Pastor Zonelia is on the right. Family on the left is who received the cow.